RICHARD MALLERY

Dr. R.V. Shrink

First edition

ISBN: 978-1-790478-82-8

This book was professionally typeset on Reedsy.
Find out more at reedsy.com

Contents

Foreword

Organ Pipe National Monument in Arizona

You can find all kinds of interesting and informative sites that tell you how to fix your RV. But only here can you be counseled on your RV frustrations. Things you never thought about when you bought that beast your driving. Like road rage (directed at you),

how to get along with your spouse in a cramped 200 sq. ft., how to get along with the camp host on a power trip. Go ahead. Ask Me! It's free counseling because you are using your own coach couch.
—Dr. R.V. Shrink

RV SHRINK, Common Sense Peddler

Introduction

My parents lived in a travel trailer after World War II. My dad worked for Michigan Bell Telephone and was moved around the state from project to project. So I guess I was conceived in an RV.

In 1956 my grandparents bought a new Airstream travel trailer. The Airstream dealer, Warner Trailer Sales, was just around the corner from our new home in Pontiac, Michigan.

A year later my dad and his brother both bought new Airstreams. We were now an Airstream family. They all became charter members of the Michigan Airstream Travel Trailer Club and we were off to rallies and camping trips every weekend.

By the late fifties, my dad had six weeks of vacation every year and he would take it all at once. Each summer we would hook onto that trailer and go off on wonderful adventures all over the country.

During my High School years, I worked for Cal Warner at the Airstream dealership. It was the largest Airstream dealer in the country at the time. Cal was a wonderful guy and

that experience truly changed my life.

It was an important time in the evolution of the RV industry. Many of our customers were executives and engineers with the Big Three, GM, Ford, and Chrysler. They were building muscle cars, not for speed but to haul heavier loads. Customers were demanding cars capable of hauling trailers. Up until that time, the standard hauler was a carryall or suburban type vehicle.

Other customers were Frank Sargent, who went on to found Thetford Corporation. He was an AC spark plug engineer always under trailers looking at plumbing fixtures. He obviously found his niche. Max Bowen (Atwood Bowen water heaters) would have me shine his Airstream once a year. He went on to design some of the first RV resorts like Disney's Fort Wilderness.

We would haul trailers from the Airstream Factory in Jackson Center, Ohio to Pontiac, Michigan with a 1964 GMC Suburban. Cal sold me the truck during my senior year in high school. My dad and I converted it into a camper and I lived in it during the summer of 1968. I have always contended that I built the first Hippie Van. In 1968, every town in the west had twenty people standing on the corner with their thumb out, looking for a ride. When I went by, they would say, "Far out man, let's get some wheels." When I got out of the Marine Corps two years later, every young person had a van painted in psychedelic colors.

I married this incredibly wonderful woman in 1974. She had traveled very little. I suggested we sell everything and travel for a year. She was all in. We bought an old Avion Travel Trailer and pulled it with the biggest frame car ever made, an Oldsmobile Custom Cruiser. We didn't come back for a decade. We laugh when people come up to us today with their chest all puffed out and tell us they are "FULL-TIMERS." We don't deflate their pride by telling them we did that forty years ago.

When our daughter was born in 1986, we expanded to a 31 ft. Airstream and traveled part of the year. Her crib was the bathtub. Our manufacturing and publishing business allowed us plenty of time to get away all through her school years. I wanted to introduce her to all the road adventures I enjoyed growing up and expand her horizons.

In 1997, I had my first book published by Doubleday. They sent us on a book tour across the country so we bought our first motorhome, a 27 ft. Jayco, Class C. We loved that rig. One afternoon on that trip we were parked at a rest area at Marias Pass in Montana. Over lunch I said to my daughter if I walked the Continental Divide from Mexico to Canada, I would cross right through this rest area. I had been dreaming of doing this for thirty years. My wife said, "Stop talking about it and let's just do it." Two summers later we did. In 1999, I hiked the entire Continental Divide from Antelope Wells, New Mexico to Waterton, Alberta, Canada. My wife and daughter were my support team in the motorhome and I would see them every two to ten days. We had a wonderful summer. Two years later we returned where I left off and continued on through the Canadian Rockies to Jasper, Alberta.

We met Chuck Woodbury years ago when we were both fledgling newspaper owners. He

published the wonderful, Out West newspaper and we The Dick E. Bird News. When Steve Jobs introduced the MacIntosh to the world we both saw an opportunity to do our own typesetting, the most expensive part of publishing at the time. It truly was one of the first "disrupters" of media.

As print slowly began to die, Chuck moved on to cyberspace, turning his newspaper into "RVtravel.com." We simply ceased printing ours after 21 years and started traveling more in our Class A Winnebago.

Eventually, Chuck suggested I publish my Dr. R.V. Shrink blog as a column in his newsletter. Now, after hundreds of columns, we are turning these columns into a series of fun and informative Ebooks. Hope you enjoy this first one.

—Keep Smilin', Dick Mallery a.k.a. Dr. R.V. Shrink

Guidance

RV big chill

Dear Dr. R.V. Shrink:

My husband is always a half bubble off plumb, or at least he thinks he is. He is a bit of a fanatic about our fifth-wheel being level. He thinks if it is the least bit off level our refrigerator will stop working. I don't see other people that concerned with being perfectly level. Will you explain to me how I can persuade him to relax and still chill?

—Cold Hearted in Henderson

Dear Cold Hearted:

Manufacturers use a more vertical design for evaporator positioning in today's cooling units. This makes it easier for evaporator coils, inside the cooling unit, to permit gravity flow of liquid ammonia through the system. Give the poor guy a break. If nothing else, his efforts will keep your refrigerator efficient and running optimally. Leveling is not the only important part of efficiency, but it is important. Being a half bubble off should not hurt a newer unit. That said, front to back and side to side leveling still remains a concern. If you run the fridge tilted for any length of time you can and will damage the cooling unit. Running off-level will cause the unit to stop circulating. I can tell you from experience that pulling a unit and having it replaced or recharged is expensive and a hassle. In the good old days, you could take the unit out and roll it, cross your fingers and sometimes get it cooling again. It's easier to do a job right than to explain why you didn't or pay for the mistake. So what's the problem. Let him be fussy, let him be precise, let him be perfectly level. If he is still a half bubble off plumb after all that, well, that would be another question and a different answer. —Keep Smilin'

The RV Lifestyle "cookin' with gas"

Dear Dr. R.V. Shrink:

My wife is a bit paranoid about a coach fire. She recently saw a YouTube video of a motorhome just like ours go up in flames on a California expressway. She seems to think ours is going to blow at any minute now. All of a sudden, propane is evil. I can't seem to convince her that this fuel source has been used safely in RVs for decades. I want to make her comfortable with our new lifestyle. How do I get her over this latest hurdle?

—Classical Gas in Garland

Dear Gasman:

I would fight fire with fire (pun intended). It is easy to find additional YouTube videos that demonstrate how safe and efficient propane is. I am sure your rig has a built-in propane detector. If for some reason it does not, you need to install one. Living in any home, fire safety should be a priority. I am shocked at how many RV owners do not realize they have escape latches on some windows, let alone how to operate them. A detector is only effective if it is charged and operating properly. A fire extinguisher

6

will only help if you know where it is, how to operate it, and has a charge. Take your wife through a "Fire Drill." It may sound like something you do with school kids, but it should be an annual event with all homeowners. Know where your shutoffs are located, what steps you will take and what order you will take them. The first thing most people do is panic. A drill is to hardwire, in your brain, the procedure you should follow. By running through a drill occasionally it will help in a real emergency to act quickly and correctly once the initial shock of an event strikes. Show your wife you are on top of all these precautionary measures. Involving her should help ease her mind. —Keep Smilin'. Dr. R.V. Shrink

Picking up our 1957 Airstream at the factory
in Jackson Center, Ohio

Hold on to your RV drawers

Dear Dr. R.V. Shrink:

My husband gets upset every time our drawer under the stove flies open. The problem is weight. I love to cook with my iron skillets. I carry three in that drawer which is a very convenient place for them. Often we will make a sharp curve and the drawer comes all the way out and falls off the slides. My husband grumbles all the time he is putting it back on and saying we should store the skillets in some other space. I do all the cooking. I don't tell him where to store his tools, so why should I have to be told where to store mine? Am I being unreasonable?

—Slip-Slidin' Away in Salerno Beach

Dear Slip:

Nothing to squabble about. Tell your husband to go out to where he keeps his tools and fetch them. Run down to the hardware and buy a childproof drawer latch and have him install it. You might want two evenly spaced depending on the weight of those iron skillets. Usually, Velcro or a second latch would be enough to hold an aggravating drawer closed, but it sounds like you are doing some heavy-duty cooking. These little problems that pop up as you fine-tune your rig are not for arguing, they are for solving to your individual tastes. Treat them as a challenge and figure out a solution by talking to others, searching online, or just putting your thinking cap on. Between now and the time you find a childproof latch, hold on to your drawers every time you round a corner.

—Keep Smilin'. Dr. R.V. Shrink

Thelma and Louise RV Adventure

Dear Dr. R.V. Shrink:

They say, "change is good", but I am not so sure. We have been enjoying the National Parks and Forests our whole life. We now see so much poor management, price gouging, and overuse, and we feel the parks are being severely depreciated. Slowly the parks are being whittled away and divvied up to the highest bidder in the public sector. We just tried to have breakfast at a concession-run cafe in Death Valley. The two women that ran the place were Thelma and Louise and seemed like they were ready to drive off a cliff at any moment. We wanted to order a basic breakfast but they were out of bacon. By the time we figured out what little they had left and decided to leave, we were already seven dollars into two cups of coffee. Then we could not get Thelma or Louise to bring us a bill, so we eventually went to the cash register to pay. At that point, both women showed up to inform us we had to wait at our table for the bill. We dropped a five and two ones and walked out. I am not writing this to complain about this breakfast experience. I am using it as a reference to the direction federal land management has taken. Thelma and Louise are just cogs in the concessioner wheel. We see a pattern of park campgrounds being taken over by private companies who then start doubling fees, charging for amenities that were once included, and delivering poor service. Isn't this just another tax on top of the taxes we already pay to have the government run our Park System? Am I the only curmudgeon traveling around grousing about this degradation? Should I just jump in the backseat with Thelma and Louise and go joy riding?
—Fuming in Furnace Creek

Dear Fuming:

I wish I could help you by waving a magic wand and solving the world's problems, but that is not going to happen. Your cure is to deal with today's challenges. Thelma and Louise are small potato problems. (Were they out of hash-browns too?) I have always said, "It's simple math - multiply numbers, divide resources." We now have 7 billion people on the planet and will move quickly to 8-9 during this next generation. That's a lot of people to manage. That's the big picture. Narrowing it down to your observations, I agree with everything you say. I have been camping in our parks and forests since the fifties. Management has evolved in lock-step with society. It has gone from Ozzie and Harriet to The Simpsons. The reasons for doling out management to concessioners, good or bad, is one of economics. Using part-time seasonal, volunteers and concessioners, these agencies cut their legacy costs and benefits, and along with that some erosion of dedication in a flux of public and private employees flowing in and out of the management of our National Treasures. This all puts our resources in jeopardy. I just spent a few days hiking the Pacific Crest Trail in the Sierra Nevada through the Granite Chief Wilderness. I was almost run over twice by mountain bikers who are banned from riding in Wilderness Areas. This was during hunting season, which should indicate a need for more management in the area, but I never saw a ranger. Obviously, the mountain bikers are also aware of this lack of supervision. Multiply this attitude exponentially and you begin to see the problems we face in protecting precious resources. Many people today want less government. As it turns out we can't afford government and government can't afford us.

—Keep Smilin'. Dr. R.V. Shrink

This is my family headed for the Seattle World's Fair in 1962—
The good looking one is our dog Duke.

RV oil change

Dear Dr. R.V. Shrink:

My husband is not a trusting person. He likes to do his own work on our motorhome when he can. When we are on the road for months at a time he would rather do his own oil changes but the parks we stay in will not allow it. We always have to find a facility that will accommodate our big rig. The little quicky places are designed for smaller vehicles. I tire of him grousing about the cost of the oil change and his worrying over what else the place might have done while under our rig. He checked after the last job and found the drain plug loose. Does everyone go through this misery or just he and me?

—Lube Brooding in Bristol

Dear Lube:

It is often a problem finding a place to work on your rig while traveling. Many of the parks that have a maintenance area only allow resident owners to use it for liability reasons. An oil change should be a fairly easy and straightforward job. I would think many parks would have an out-of-the-way place for you to do such a quick procedure as long as you were careful to catch your drained oil and dispose of it properly. I have never found it a problem, and I change mine every three thousand miles. I always put a tarp down as insurance against any accidental spills, and most auto specialty stores will take your used oil. If you use a service facility, you should give them specific instructions on what you want to be done and check the drain plug and filter when the job is finished. Many facilities offer a plethora of services accompanying the oil change that you may not want them fooling with. Be specific. If a park does not allow this procedure it may be they have had issues in the past with people leaving a mess. It is no different from businesses offering free parking lot overnight stays. One bad apple can spoil the barrel. We have seen where people have dumped their gray water in Walmart parking lots. It would only take one person to create a mini-oil spill to turn a park owner or manager sour on trying to work with those who want to do a little precautionary maintenance.

—Keep Smilin'. Dr. R.V. Shrink

RV smoke signals

Dear Dr. R.V. Shrink:

We were recently at a commercial RV park in Arizona with terrible Wi-Fi reception. We specifically chose this park because it advertised Wi-Fi. We paid for a week before we realized the Wi-Fi was only available if you sat on the bench outside the office. My husband spent a hundred dollars on some crazy device that was supposed to reach out and grab the signal. It worked to some degree, but I would rather have a hundred bucks than mediocre Wi-Fi. The park had many permanent residents with a separate internet service. Near the end of our stay, a guy came over to talk to my husband. He was trying to figure out if we were getting on their internet and if we had their password. My husband was trying to help him with the password that was given to us by the park office and told him about the receiver thingy he had bought. As the conversation continued my husband finally figured out the guy knew more than he did about this techie stuff. He was actually one of the residents on the separate service and thought we were stealing their Wi-Fi. I thought it a bit rude for him to come over and pretend he needed help. We can hardly spell Wi-Fi let alone hack into someone else's signal. I'm sure I had smoke coming out my ears when I realized what was going on, but I held my tongue. When we left we felt like people had probably been watching us suspiciously for days and treating us like criminals, when we were actually the ones who paid for a service we never received. I don't really have a question, I just wanted to let off steam.

—Smoke Signals in Sedona

Dear Smokey:

Many parks have discovered that Wi-Fi is very important to

customers. Putting in an adequate system to cover a park and supply the data is not cheap, but many parks are investing in better coverage. There is no such thing as a "free lunch." You will often pay more for this service, cable or any other amenity. Like your husband and many other readers, I have tried several signal boosting, long-range adapters such as those produced by Alfa Networks. They work to some degree, but often the park is putting out a weak signal and it is only meant for guests to use at the clubhouse or near the office. It can be frustrating for those who share a connection with others. If someone is streaming video it can throttle everyone else. Your guy should be looking at members of his own group. I assume they have their network password protected, so someone in his group must be giving it out. You might want to call ahead or ask more specific questions when you reach a park before you reach for your wallet. Some parks will use language like, "Wi-Fi Available." Sometimes that means you can buy short-term service from a nearby provider. Sometimes that means you have to be parked next to the office pointing SE, up on one wheel and hold your computer over your head next to the slide-out window. A Long-Range USB Adapter will only let you see a signal and sometimes tell you its strength. It will not let you access data if it is protected, as most are. Those little "receiver thingy's" are great in certain situations, but you can't count on them all the time. I met a guy who hooked one up to a Pringles can. It wasn't working so I told him to try two soup cans and tie them together with a long string. He just gave me the stink eye.

—Keep Smilin', Dr. R.V. Shrink

1950's Vintage models at Apgar Campground in Glacier National Park, Montana

Jesse James RV Repair Service

Dear Dr. R.V. Shrink:

I know you have covered breaking down on the road in the past. I read your advice carefully. I always wondered how we would fare if we had to deal with a major problem during our several months away from home. At home, we are familiar with area service people or have enough friends for recommendations. On the road, it is not so easy. Now we see, with Amazon's recent lawsuits, that people can be paid to give online reviews. We recently had engine problems. We asked people in the park and the management who they would recommend, checked online reviews for those we could, and we still got ripped off.

—So low in Show Low

Dear So low:

Life's a crapshoot and an adventure. You can do all the preparation in the world, but sooner or later you have to throw the dice. I can answer with a personal experience. Just recently our Saturn transmission decided to start shifting with a clunk. Sounded like a sledgehammer hitting a rail spike. We were staying at an SKP Park on the Olympic Peninsula in Washington. I could drive it carefully if I stayed in second. When we returned to the park I asked management and a few permanent residents for a recommendation. I went online and read many reviews. My first thought was to find someone local. I also Googled my problem on several online forums. I made a list of several shops in a 50-mile radius and started interviewing. That's right, they were going to go to work for me. I wanted someone nice, polite, competent and honest. Everyone I talked to seemed to fit the bill. They were all nice, polite, seemed competent and all had the same diagnosis. From my online studies, it sounded like the transmission valve body needed replacing. Everyone I talked to seemed to agree. I finally made a couple choices and decided to haul the car to the transmission shops with the motorhome. I picked two places about 40 miles away in close proximity to each other. If I didn't like the first one I could move on for a second opinion. The first guy was really nice. Took the car in immediately, ran the electronic codes, test drove the car and told me I needed to have the whole transmission rebuilt. He had so many code errors my car should have died three years ago. For just under three thousand bucks he could have me back on the road in about a week. That's when it hit me. Railroad employees always used to say that Jesse James was nice and always polite, but he still took all their money. I paid them $52 for their advice and moved on. When I was leaving the guy said, "Reverse doesn't work very well." I said, "That's okay, I'm not coming back." By the time I hauled the car to the next place it was four o'clock in the afternoon. I was hoping they could at least take a look at it before they closed. It was at a business called Tranco Transmissions in Port Angeles, Washington. It looked very clean and organized. In fact, I think you could eat off the floor. They brought me right in, and let me watch them as they plugged the code reader into my car. Surprise! There were no error codes. They said that 95% of the time it is just the valve body gone bad. They could order one (out of state) and have it there by the next morning. With the hour they had before closing they could have the old one off and ready for the new one in the morning. I would be "Back on the Road Again" for $752. I pulled the trigger, "Let's do it." Went out for Chinese dinner, spent a quiet, beautiful night in Olympic National Park and the car was ready for pickup by nine o'clock the next morning. My old Saturn is now purring like a tomcat in a creamery. It pays to be a little suspect. Stories do not always have a happy ending, but if you go through the motions, control your emotions and dial out all the commotions, you have a better chance than being treated like lambs to the slaughter. Chalk your recent adventure up to experience and move on.

—Keep Smilin', Dr. R.V. Shrink

More power to the RV relationship

Dear Dr. R.V. Shrink:

We agree with you and love our solar power setup. However,

we are seldom hooked to the grid. On occasion, we will get too many overcast days to keep our batteries topped off. When that happens it takes us a long time to recoup even if we plug in. My husband wants to spend over three hundred dollars for a 50 amp battery charger. He says it will enable him to quickly recharge our 4—6volt golf cart batteries when we use the generator or plug into the grid. This situation only occurs a couple times a year as we are usually in a sunny clime. The disagreement is this: I think we should invest those 300+ dollars into more solar panels or more battery storage. My husband is a great guy and knows a lot more than I do about these things. I don't want to come across as a know-it-all. Am I missing something, or am I a common sense genius?

—Powerplay in Pahrump

Dear PP:

Don't pooh-pooh your ideas just because you might be stepping on your husband's expertise. You are getting the "love of power" confused with the "power of love." The great thing about having a partnership relationship is input. This question involves many different decisions— budget, investment, solution and agreement to mention a few. I can't make the decision for you. You both are on the right track. Your husband is right about a more powerful charger. Most RV converters act as a trickle charger. The fact that you say it takes a long time to recoup suggests your converter fits this category. In defense of your common sense idea, I would have to agree. If I were going to invest the money, I would rather have panels that were paying me back year-round, than a charger getting me out of trouble a couple times a year. However, adding panels and batteries can be challenging if you do not have space. Also, a decent 50 battery charger/maintainer can be had for fifty bucks. If you only deal with this low battery problem a couple times a year, it tells me there is no abuse of power in your household. I think the same can be said for your relationship.

—Keep Smilin', Dr. R.V. Shrink

Friends around the Casita at Gilbert Ray County Park
near Tucson and Saguaro National Monument

Strapped for RV space

Dear Dr. R.V. Shrink:

My husband and I have a lot of toys. We travel full-time hauling bikes, kayaks, diving gear, golf clubs, tennis rackets, backpacking gear, and now a drone. We look like the Clampett's going down the road with stuff tied and clamped everywhere. It doesn't bother my husband, but I would like to have something a bit more organized. I think we should buy a big motorhome with basement storage, but he likes the unit we have. He argues we have everything figured out with this one. He solved all the storage problems with bungees, and he knows where everything is. I call it his "pile file." He now wants one of those fold up boats you tie to the side of the motorhome. I have been fighting that because every time we put the slides out we would have to dock the boat somewhere else. I need help Doc, and I need it fast. He is on the computer right now looking at bungees in bulk.

—Stretched in Stratford

Dear Stretched:

Let me begin with a bumper sticker I saw that said, "He who dies with the most toys WINS!" It sounds like you two have lots of interests, an active, healthy lifestyle, and a storage problem. Since you backpack, I'm sure you've seen people on the trail with a pack full of gear, and more strapped and tied to the outside that just will not stuff inside. That would be you on steroids. Many people make this work, but the advantages of organizing it all inside under cover are many. Anything that will fit in, or undercover, will benefit from protection against the elements. That said, basement storage will come with the cost and hassle of switching rigs to gain that organized space. If you pull a toad, you might want to consider something larger with storage capacity, if you haven't already. Some people prefer to rent equipment when they visit an area, but that rarely works out for spontaneous activity. It puts you on the rental company's schedule and geographical location. You should consider the safety issues involved in tying equipment to every bracket you can attach to on your rig. I have seen rigs going down the road with equipment tied to the roof ladder that made me back way off. Many of these ladders are simply screwed to the frame and not engineered to carry a heavy load. Bungees can, and often do, fail. How many do you see on the road as you travel? Weight distribution is also an important safety factor. Some people think they can save on tire wear by strapping a Harley on the rear bumper to keep the front tires off the ground. Many people start out their RV adventure with a rig that fits their needs at the time. Soon they discover it is too big or too small. Others find they don't have all the amenities they would like, or it has too darn many. Your situation is no different. Maybe you should look into a Toy Hauler fifth-wheel. They come with their own garage.

—Keep Smilin', Dr. R.V. Shrink

Power to the RV people

Dear Dr. R.V. Shrink:

My husband wants to spend a couple grand on a solar panel system for our fifth-wheel. He complains every time our lights go dim while dry camping. We had to leave Big Bend National Park early because we were out of battery power. It was cold and we had to run the furnace every morning. The furnace fan seems to suck a lot of juice from our batteries. I argue that we can buy a lot of full hookups for two grand. He is not listening. He is too busy studying the solar system. I tell him he has stars in his eyes. Do you think I am being unreasonable, frugal or cheap?

—Powerless in El Paso

Dear Powerless:

It really depends on how often you dry camp. You can easily

pay for a system in a year if you dry camp the majority of the time. Because so many RVs now have solar, many parks will have a reduced rate if you do not want to plug in. Some Arizona State Parks will reduce the rate and lock the electrical box if you opt out of the electric. Yes, the furnace fan is a power hog. Another option would be to install a catalytic heater such as an Olympian Wave. They put out a very nice radiant heat without the need for a fan. You can recess mount it or use a long hose with a disconnect to enable you to move it around. I am solar biased, but it really depends on how you use your RV. If you seldom dry camp, solar is probably a waste of money. You will start to see more manufacturers offering a solar option. They need little maintenance, give you quiet, continuous power, and as Elon Musk recently said, "We have this handy fusion reactor in the sky, called the Sun." Another point to be made is the fact that many RVs now come standard with a generator that people put few hours on. For the same money, you can put on a very efficient solar system. If you can live with the 12v power that is generated, it will not be necessary to spend another thousand or so for an expensive inverter. You can buy small inverters (400 watts) that are capable of running a coffee grinder, recharge computers or power an electric razor. You can easily add up your energy needs and see if it is a good investment, a fun project or a worthwhile convenience. You are not going to run an electric heater or refrigerator from a small RV solar array. They have their limitations. I can tell you from experience that once you can live within the means of a 300-watt system it will set you free. LED lights can also be a good, long-term investment that will extend your Big Bend, out of the way stay. And don't forget CONSERVATION, it gives "power to the people."

—Keep Smilin', Dr. R.V. Shrink

My first RV—Built into a 1964 suburban—Backpacking through Western North America, summer of 1968

Wishy Washy RVer

Dear Dr. R.V. Shrink:

One of the drudgeries of RVing is finding a decent place to do laundry. They are often expensive, poorly managed, dirty and/or busy. I think we should have a washer/dryer in our motorhome, but my husband thinks it's a bad idea. We share the laundry duty, but he thinks a machine will take up too much space and add too much weight for the convenience it will afford us. It just sounds so sensible to me. Don't you think the full-time lifestyle deserves a guaranteed, clean and personal machine to wash our clothing?

—Wishy Washy in Wilmington

Dear Wishy Washy:

I will agree that finding a clean, affordable laundromat on the road is a constant challenge. Most often you are better served using a commercial campground laundry that is used only by paying guests. If the park is highly rated, you will usually find the laundry facilities reasonable, clean and much less busy. I have nothing against a washer/dryer combination installed in an RV. Many of them have a very small load capacity and take a lot of time to cycle. It does allow you to work on the chore at your convenience and not let it all pile up for a trip to the mat. These units will also suck your water tank dry, so if you are not hooked up to utilities you will find yourself needing fresh water and a dump much more often. If you decide against an onboard unit, another thought is Googling the laundromat you plan to use. You will often find sites like Yelp and TripAdvisor rating such businesses. The problems with using machines that you find in public parks, such as state and local, can be frustrating. If it rains you will find wet campers throwing their dirty bags and tents into dryers. At fishing sites, you may find your clothes come out smelling like the day's catch. If you come to an onboard agreement you should weigh the difference between a separate washer/dryer or a combination machine. They can usually be installed in a closet and your unit might even be plumbed for it if you check. Another alternative is "The John Steinbeck Method." If you read "Travels with Charley" you will discover that Steinbeck, one of our more prolific literary laundrymen, used a plastic garbage can hanging from bungies to do his wash. He would let the road do his agitating as he meandered across America. Wash all morning, add the rinse water at noon and hang and dry when he stopped. Not a bad idea and you save yourself about a grand in machine costs.

—Keep Smilin'. Dr. R.V. Shrink

I'm going to Disney World—NOT!

Dear Dr. R.V. Shrink:

We are in the mouse house and I am not talking about Disney World. We just spent a week parked at Many Glacier campground near Babb, Montana. It is starting to feel like fall here and the mice decided they would like to go to Arizona with us. We trapped five last night. The cat caught two, and we still hear gnawing in the underbelly of our trailer. I want to use d-Con but my wife hates poison and says it is cruel. That sounds Dopey to me. She thinks a quickly broken neck is much more humane. Isn't dead, dead? How can I convince her that we need to take decisive, defensive action before we are overrun with vermin? I'm not getting much sleep lately. In the middle of the night the cat catches a mouse, my wife catches the cat, and they both run outside until the cat drops the mouse. I think at that point the mouse beats them both back to the trailer. This is our full-time home. Help me.

—Grumpy and in Babb

Dear Babb:

As tight as an RV seems to be, mice can wiggle their way in. It is a problem that must be dealt with quickly before wiring is chewed, material is collected for nesting, food stores are cached, and plumbing tubing is damaged. They can do a tremendous amount of damage in a very short time. I agree with your wife, poison is not your best solution. d-Con is designed to drive the mice out to water after it starts its deadly process. These poison carcasses will move their way up the food chain very quickly as other predators find them, harming things that do not want to travel with you. You will often find the mice have stored it all over the RV and never eaten it. You need to continue running your trapline and know you have eliminated the last one. At this point, you don't know how "Minnie" Mickeys you have. You will most likely be able to tell you have solved the problem when the cat stops acting Goofy. Don't forget to tie a string to every trap and secure it to something. Even after the trap does it's deadly deed, the mouse will dance a distance. If it ends up in a place you cannot reach it will decay and begin to smell. Once you get the situation under control you can try home remedies like peppermint tea bags (they hate the smell). For now, I would stick to playing cat and mouse and using cheese and traps. Remember, the pioneers got the arrows and the settlers got the land. Same applies here. The second mouse gets the cheese, so use several traps. The only positive thing you can take from this experience is the fact that this is the most excitement your cat has had in a long time. Living in a small RV is not easy for a cat, even if it sleeps eighteen hours a day. It has most likely raised your cat's spirits, given your cat much-needed exercise, and made your cat feel like the Lion King. Seriously, set traps everywhere and deal with this problem immediately, before it gets really expensive.

—Keep Smiling,' Dr. R.V. Shrink

Counsel

RV Phone Home

Dear Dr. R.V. Shrink:

We are going to begin our RV adventure this fall. My husband and I are both newly retired and almost ready to head out, beginning with a fall color tour through the Rockies. We have been in almost perfect agreement on every issue leading up to departure until now. We are trying to decide on a service provider for our phones and wireless needs. My husband thinks we need two smartphones, a hotspot with a couple dozen gigs of data and two different service providers. I think that is overkill and a waste of money. I know you are always suggesting the use of online data for everything from dump stations to gas stations, but do we really need that much coverage? Besides the data, we just need to phone home once in a while. Please give us some of your common sense therapy.

—ET in D.C.

Dear ET:

This is a really common concern for people starting out on the road. It also varies for each individual. Expense, affordability, need and desire can be all over the data scale. I would suggest you look at what you use at home. This is only a starting point because

DR. R.V. SHRINK

you will most likely need more on the road if you both are heavy computer users. I constantly look for a better deal than I have and switch when it is advantageous. We are grandfathered into an old Alltel plan that Verizon bought out. We get 20 gigs for what most people pay for 5 gigs. That sounds like a lot of data, but we use it every single month. We don't stream movies or watch much video, which eats up a lot of data. We do watch Nightly News if we cannot get a TV channel, which is most of the time. I have a dumb phone and my wife has a smartphone. We cannot tether it, but that is an option if you use the right service and the right phone manufacturer. My wife has a Walmart Straight Talk plan with a Samsung phone and a Verizon chip. For under fifty bucks a month she gets unlimited talk, text, and data. It works almost everywhere we travel. We have RV friends that have Straight Talk, AT&T service and an HTC phone, and they are able to use the phone as a hotspot. Again, unlimited everything. We were told we would be throttled occasionally if we used too much data, but after a year we have not noticed that ever happening. You can start out with what you currently have and work up to what you feel you need as you travel. I can guarantee that you will more than pay for data service, in savings you will realize, using the many cheap and often free apps that direct you to fuel, camping, dumping, road construction, directions, and ME, of course!

—Keep Smilin', Dr. R.V. Shrink

RV Road Less Traveled

Dear Dr. R.V. Shrink:

Are we the only ones who always seem to choose the wrong routes? We like to stay off the major highways and see rural

28

America, but we are always in some kind of trouble. Last month we had to unhook our toad and make a U-turn at a low overpass. Today we spent over two hours along 30 miles of North Dakota road construction that were worse than anything we experienced on the Alcan Highway 30 years ago before it was paved. We are not sure if the North Dakota Department of Transportation is in charge out here or the "fracking" companies. We had dropped off Hwy. 2 in Stanley, ND, heading for the Theodore Roosevelt National Park, North Unit, and there was no indication that our route was a virtual nightmare. There were no detour signs, no flag people, inaccurate mileage signs and narrow passage points. This seems to be a pattern for us. Are we poor navigators, or does everyone deal with situations like this?
—Newbies trying to learn in North Dakota

Dear Newbies:

I applaud your sense of adventure — keep it up. The alternative is staying on boring, exit-laden, superhighways and reading billboards. There are a few things you can do to alleviate some of your headaches. Many GPS systems have major construction updates and low clearance warnings. You can make a habit of asking locals when you make pit stops to see if you can garner any information about possible surprises ahead of you. Some companies like AAA are well known for travel map information that is very up-to-date. With all that said, I still go back to using today's technology as your best source of information. Services may be out-of-date, locals may be ill-informed, signs, as you well know, can be deceiving. As far as who is in charge of the new hot fracking areas, that could fuel a great debate. So much activity and new infrastructure make some of my old stomping grounds look unrecognizable. I just asked Dr. Google for North Dakota road conditions. I was directed to the Dept. of Trans. North Dakota site. There I found a state map. On it I found your route lit up like a Christmas Tree. When I clicked on the construction site it warned of "poor road conditions." If you would have stayed on Hwy. 2 you wouldn't have a tale to tell. Now you have this great campfire story and it only cost you a bit of slow going and maybe an RV wash. Chances are you will hit as much construction or more on major travel arteries than you will on the back roads of America. Keep doing what you enjoy and deal with the challenges.

—Keep Smilin', Dr. R.V.Shrink

Happiness is the spectacular Grand Tetons
out the RV window at breakfast

Cat in the RV Hat

Dear Dr. R.V. Shrink:

We live in a moderately sized motorhome most of the year. At the present time, we have one cat on board. We love this little furball, but he does cause a lot of anxiety. He also causes a lot of arguments. I seem to be more attached to him than my husband. He enjoys the cat but doesn't enjoy the hassles that come with pet ownership. Our biggest problem is playing "Hide and Go Seek." Every time we pull up anchor and set sail, the little bugger hides. We spend a lot of time trying to find him so I am assured he hasn't jumped out. This last time he was wedged under the front dash. This drives my husband nuts because I won't leave until I know my cat is safe. Is this asking too much? He gets as much companionship from the cat as I do. I would love to hear your take on our situation.

—Cat Calling in Calgary

Dear Cal:

Traveling with pets has its pros and cons. It should be decided upfront if the companionship is worth the effort involved in taking proper care of your animal(s). They can crimp your style if you want to be absent for any length of time. They have to be fed, watered, exercised and cleaned up after. These are all responsibilities that are required if you live in an RV or not. It is obvious that you have already discussed these matters and came to some type of decision because you have a cat on board. I am an expert on "cat search and rescue" missions. I have been on many in campgrounds all over America. Our last cat was self-taught. She learned how to slide the screen open and jump out. Many times we gave up trying to find her. In a sea of RVs, she would always find her way home, climb up the ladder to the roof and cry at the vent. We finally had to tape the screens shut. Hiding is a cat thing. I think you should just allow time to do a thorough cat scan before traveling. Put it on your departure list. It is no different than waiting for the jacks to go up, or insuring the awning is down. Our cat likes to climb in any cupboard or closet we leave open. So checking to make sure the cat is in sight even if you leave for a short hike will assure you never have a cat-astrophe. (Sorry, I couldn't help myself.) Pets can add a lot of joy to your life if you have the right attitude toward them. That means both of you. A little give-and-take will solve a lot of small problems that seem more complicated than they are. Our newest cat has never escaped and seems to have no desire to jump out. When they constantly have that urge, they can be much more challenging. Hiding in the coach is a much easier problem to deal with. Once you know all the usual places it's as easy as finding a two-year-old. Let's not forget the financial pains of pet medical care. We just spent $328 to find out our cat had the "Big C." Yup, he was Constipated!

—Keep Smilin', Dr. R.V. Shrink

RV tail gunner

Dear Dr. R.V. Shrink:

My husband gets so upset when driving our motorhome all day. He is constantly talking to people that annoy him and it gets on my nerves. Someone is always doing something stupid in his opinion. It doesn't make traveling pleasant when he is grousing all the time. He does all the driving and I sometimes think I should let him vent, but it gets old after a while. He says some pretty obnoxious things. Do you think I should sit quietly by while he goes through his ranting or continue to work on administering anger management?

—Annoyed in Annapolis

Dear Annoyed:

There is a big difference between driving all day and riding all day. Nowadays a driver has to be alert and driving defensively every minute. That can lead some people to fatigue and anxiety. There are so many fellow drivers on their smart phones texting or with their heads up their Apps that if you aren't paying attention constantly you might be their next contact. If you can't put up with your husband's constant vocalizations, you might want to buy him one of those steering wheel sound simulators. With the pressing of a couple of buttons, he can fire a burst of machine gun fire, a rocket launcher or short bursts of sniper fire. This would let him vent his anger without loud, R-rated outbursts. Although this may drive you crazier! Part of compatible traveling includes understanding your traveling partner's needs, wants, dislikes and idiosyncrasies. Working together to meet in the middle of an issue will take you a long way into the realm of Happy Camperdom. Keep working on his anger management, be a supportive co-pilot and eventually, he will mellow, knowing it bothers you. I just had another thought. You could work together: He can be the pilot, and you can be the tail gunner.

—Keep Smilin'. Dr. R.V. Shrink

Taking on water at Devils Tower National Monument, Wyoming

RV Corps of Discovery

Dear Dr. R.V. Shrink:

We found your articles while surfing the web. We are thinking about buying an RV and traveling like so many others. Our biggest question seems to be how much money it costs to live on the road. Can you give us some idea of the expenses we might encounter? Is there a rule of thumb, like the 4% rule of making a retirement nest egg last and not outliving your money? Any input would be greatly appreciated.

—Bean Counter in Bend

Dear Bean Counter:

One size does not fit all. You can't lump everyone's RV cost of living budgets into one figure, any more than you can lump together the sedentary lifestyle cost of living budgets. Wherever you weigh in on the financial scale you can find a niche in the RV lifestyle. Put pen to paper and create a road budget. It is so easy to find regional costs online for fuel, camping, maintenance, food, and services. You should be able to calculate your capabilities into a travel scenario that fits the ideas you have. From the type of rig, you plan to travel with, to the type of camping you plan to do, will make a huge difference in your cost of living. You may not get it right the first time, but the experience will reveal to you the possibilities of a nomadic lifestyle that fits your interests, needs, and means. So many people never get out of the driveway because of the unknown. The adventure is the unknown. The steeper the learning curve the more fun it is. Once you get it all figured out it becomes less exciting. There are many sayings that originated with the flintlock rifle. They are all well suited to beginning a life on the road in an RV. "Going off half-cocked, " "Flash in the pan," "Straight as a ramrod," Lock stock and barrel," and "Keep your powder dry." These come to mind because we met a couple just beginning their own RV lifestyle at Fort Clatsop, the winter encampment for the Corps of Discovery. It was their first volunteer job and they were doing reenactments. All those sayings were part of their program. I thought how ironic, Lewis and Clark, two of the first North American explorers, are being historically represented by modern day North American explorers. So do your homework and come join the rest of us in the Corps of Discovery.

—Keep Smilin', Dr. R.V. Shrink

RV forecasting

Dear Dr. R.V. Shrink:

I need scheduling help. My wife is refusing to camp in certain areas. With all the drought in the West, the news is full of fires and floods. I told her the TV broke because one more night of news and we will have to start camping at fire stations across America for her to feel safe and know help is close by. Just when I thought I had her convinced she was overreacting, our Glacier National Park campground reservation was canceled for Lake St. Mary Campground. A fire was threatening the area and we were not allowed in. I tried to explain to her that we live on wheels and can move at the drop of a hat if things looked sketchy wherever we camp. Now my every suggestion is suspect. It is driving me nuts. Should I buy a fire truck and convert it into an RV? It would already have a large fresh water holding tank. Do you think that would make her feel safer?

—Disaster Dave in Deer Lodge

Dear Dave in Deer Lodge:

There is nothing wrong with preparedness. Worry and stress are another issues. I heard that "there is nothing to fear but fear itself." Traveling to avoid everything you see on the news will limit you to a padded cell. I can see how your wife works herself into a frenzy. I was watching Nightly News last week when I saw a 5th wheel float down a road in Wickenburg, Arizona. Keeping your head in the sand will not solve any problems. Information is the key to safety. I would suggest you camp where you want but have a backup plan. Know your escape routes, incoming weather events, fire conditions, and terrain. Words from a sage much wiser than myself fit here perfectly. Forrest Gump sums it up with two of his famous quotes: "Stupid is as stupid does." (This would be good advice for people who put themselves in harm's way, ignoring the conditions.) Also, "My momma always said, 'Life was like a box of chocolates. You never know what you're gonna get.'" (This would be to emphasize the fact that you have to be prepared for anything.) There are five other campgrounds in Glacier still open. One is a reservation campground and the others are first come, first serve. Think of a change in plans as an adventure. You may discover something new and enjoyable because your original plans were altered by conditions out of your control. When you think about it, you only have a few conditions to worry about — wind, heavy rain, hail, tornado, fire, flood, hurricane, earthquake, tsunami, blizzard, sandstorm and maybe a dust devil or two.

—Keep Smilin', Dr. R.V. Shrink

An office with a window—The Window Trail,
Big Bend National Park, Texas

That blew that RV theory

Dear Dr. R.V. Shrink: It is not nice to fool Mother Nature, or fool
with her. Don't you think you should be more careful stating that
you can always leave at the drop of a hat during a natural disaster?
   —R.V. Shrink

Dear Me:
   Yes, I am writing to myself. It's okay, I have been talking to
myself for years.

After reading the Shrink column above, you see my advice on trying to foresee coming natural disasters and moving out of harm's way. In my feeble attempt to be funny I closed with, "When you think about it, you only have a few conditions to worry about — wind, heavy rain, hail, tornado, fire, flood, hurricane, earthquake, tsunami, blizzard, sandstorm and maybe a dust devil or two." Well, I left out Mesocyclone and the very next day Mother Nature reminded me. We were at the Traverse City, Michigan Film Festival, inside an auditorium, watching the new documentary film, "A Brave Heart, The Lizzie Velasquez Story" (which I highly recommend). Unbeknown to us a vicious storm was raging outside the auditorium. We emerged to a street full of broken trees covering broken cars. Our car was parked a block away and we hurried to find our vehicle unscathed but surrounded by downed branches big enough to heat a house for a winter. It was a labyrinth working our way out of town. We were turned back several times by large trees blocking roads. We passed the Traverse City State Park and it looked like a box of broken matchsticks. We could see a pop-up camper crushed and feared we may be headed for the same kind of surprise. Our motorhome was parked in an open area next to a couple large trees that had the potential to do damage. Luckily we found our rig intact. Although a couple dozen trees had been broken or uprooted within 50 yards in all directions of our motorhome, nothing had come close to causing us damage. The point I want to make is, you can run, but you cannot hide. This storm came in so silently and quickly that there was no choice but to ride it out, wherever you were, and to find safety wherever you could. This has little to do with whether you RV or not. Disaster can strike anywhere and at anytime. This whole region of Northwest Michigan has been reeling from this storm, and its aftermath, all week. Our next stop is Glacier National Park and the fire there is still burning. You just have to roll with the punches, be as careful as possible and hope for the best. Last year, at the Winnebago factory in Iowa, a beautiful motorhome pulled in next to us with cannonball-size dents, broken windows, and hundreds of chips in the full paint finish. They had run straight into a storm dropping large hail. There is no way to ever predict this type of event. It is the reason we all have insurance coverage. Do not let the possibility of something like this scare you from a life of adventure on the great open road. If you don't go out and find a storm, one will come looking for you. Either way, you will have to deal with it.

—Keep Smilin', Dr. R.V. Shrink

RV Looney Tunes

Dear Dr. R.V. Shrink:

I don't mean to be an annoyance, but I need more help. I wrote a few weeks ago about my husband not fixing the hot water heater that was singing to me. Since I last wrote, my husband spent several hours and dollars trying to fix our hot water heater as you suggested. He couldn't get the element to unscrew and finally sought professional help which was not cheap. I hate to sound like a broken record, but the hot water heater is still singing to me. This time it's a different tune and a whole lot worse. The sound comes from the tank every time I turn on the hot water. I hesitated to bring this issue up with my husband. He is still agitated by the last episode. To my surprise, he brought it up. The noise seems to be bugging him also. We are five hundred miles away from where we had the element changed. My husband called them and they said it was not the element. They suggested we now need new "check valves." Is our hot water heater possessed? Are we getting scammed? Should we just play loud music all the time to drown out the water heater noise? Please send more advice our way.

—Sounding Board, no longer in Bozeman

Dear Boze, again:

You are not getting scammed. It is also a common occurrence to have check valves start making noise. Perhaps something was flushed into one when the element work was done. Regardless, it is another simple fix. If your husband doesn't feel confident doing plumbing work, you might want to have another repair shop handle it. Depending on the model hot water heater and RV floor plan, it can be quick and easy or a real pain. It is usually all about access. I am imagining your husband trying to get the element out. It can be challenging. The last time I tackled mine, it was a task. It is on the inside, backside of the heater, which meant taking part of the under cabinet apart to reach. Most people find the element very hard to budge. The element nut is very thin and hard to grip. The often sold, thin-walled element socket is not really the best tool for the job. I use a regular inch and a half, six-point socket that fits my half-inch ratchet. It allows me much more leverage. Even with that, I had to use my torch to heat the tank wall before it would budge. You will find one or two check valves on the backside of your tank. They should loosen a bit easier than the element. The valves that often come with your unit have plastic inserts. I would recommend you switch them out with brass. So here is the bottom line. Your husband can go to another professional and spend one hundred plus dollars to silence the hot water heater or take a crack at it himself. It means taking one or two water lines loose, extracting the valve(s), replacing them, and hooking up the water lines again. I like to think of these little annoyances as an adventure. You also get more acquainted with your rig and have a better understanding of how it all works. Don't be afraid to tackle these jobs. There will always be something that needs tweaking, so don't turn them all into mountains, they are just molehills.

—Keep Smilin'. Dr. R.V. Shrink

The RV Lifestyle comes in all shapes and sizes
Home is where you haul it!

RV Chairman of the Road

Dear Dr. R.V. Shrink:

I don't know who engineers motorhomes, but they need to work on TV placement. When we were shopping for our rig we finally gave up finding one with a TV located in a comfortable place for viewing. The problem is my husband solved the problem by purchasing one of those outdoor, reclining La-Z-Boy-type chairs to put in the hallway facing the TV. Even though we have a slide-out, it still leaves no room for moving around. Once we get in our positions (me on the couch, he in his chair) to watch a movie, there is no getting up for popcorn without a major shift in furniture. I think we should get him a chair that takes up less real estate, but he likes his new recliner. The motorhome is small enough already. I don't think I am asking too much to have the walkway clear. Your opinion would be much appreciated.

—Hall Monitor in Manchester

Dear Hall Monitor:

I do agree that many RVs are engineered with the TV taking up whatever space might be left after all other appliances have been placed. Some models have two to four televisions and they all seem to be in an awkward location. Besides the space that your husband's chair takes up, it sounds like a great idea. Perhaps he could find a similar model in a smaller frame. I don't think that is asking too much. Another idea would be to relocate the TV or invest in a portable that could be placed in a position that would make viewing comfortable for your particular floor plan. Depending on the amount of time you spend watching TV programming, you might want to consider using a laptop computer to watch movies or news. Another thought would be to shop TV mount options.

Some allow swivel positioning side to side and up and down. If you can wait a bit longer, LG is coming out with a TV that is only 0.97mm thick. It will stick to the wall like a fridge magnet. Maybe Google Glass will allow you to watch in the side frame of your glasses, sitting anywhere you, please. What will they think of next to entertain couch potatoes?

—Keep Smilin', Dr. R.V. Shrink

Down in the RV dumps

Dear Dr. R.V. Shrink:

In our relationship, my husband is the RV technician and I am the cook. If I were the RV technician nothing would work, and if he were the cook we would starve. In our respective specialties, we get to make certain decisions that affect our daily lives. This has always worked out fine. Since recently moving into a small motorhome things have changed in both departments. I cook simpler meals, and he hauls fewer tools. Everything seemed to flow smoothly in our new lifestyle until I was advised we could no longer deposit any solids into our new RV holding tank. My husband told me it would mound up in the tank and clog the outlet. We are now inconvenienced with running to the campground public restrooms. I find some of them rather disgusting. I don't want him telling me how to cook, but I question his decision on the toilet. Why would millions of RVs have toilets and holding tanks designed into them if they were not usable? How should I approach this question without stepping on his turf?

—Down in the dumps in Dawson

Dear Dawson:

As odd as it sounds each time I hear it, this practice is not uncommon. Many people seem to have a hangup with using the toilet in their RV the same way they would anywhere else. In some cases perhaps they watched Robin Williams dump his "RV" in the movie with the same name and developed a phobia. Some I have asked feel RV toilets are not engineered well enough to flush out solids and therefore create constant blockages. Others simply find it disgusting to have to deal with the doo. You will have to figure out which category your husband falls into before you can solve your problem permanently. If it is a simple phobia issue, you can help solve that by volunteering to take on this simple and sanitary chore yourself. If it's an engineering question you will only have to give him a few lines of instruction to solve all doubt. Your husband is right. If not managed properly, solids can mound in the tank and clog outlets. There are certain precautions that must be taken from dump to dump. You must start with a few bowls of water in the tank. Do not flush solids into a dry tank. Adding some septic safe chemicals can help break down solids, suppress odors and lubricate slide valves. Another important point is tissue type. You want it to dissolve quickly. Buy tissue designed for RV holding tanks or test the brand you choose by sloshing it around in a jar of water. It should quickly disintegrate into small specks of thin tissue. Whatever it does in that jar of water is exactly what it will do in your holding tank. The tank emptying procedure is also very important. Having a tank near full when you empty is ideal. If it is not and you have access to water, fill it. It's simple physics, or math if you prefer. An abundance of No. 1 (liquid) will help eliminate No. 2 (solids). Pressure and gravity equal a forceful flush. One common mistake people make is leaving the blackwater valve open when hooked to a campground sewer. This immediately empties the tank of liquids and leaves the solids to accumulate and harden in the tank. Precautionary maintenance in the form of knowledgeable fill and emptying procedure should give you trouble-free use of the RV toilet facilities. Having the right equipment (rubber gloves, hoses, connectors, hand sanitizer, and assorted fittings) should make dumping the holding tanks quick, sanitary, and efficient. It should not be a gender-specific job. Like everything else when dealing with RV living, everyone should be prepared to handle all duties. Perhaps your husband should attempt a quiche, while you practice sanitary engineering. The old dirty-swirly is not as difficult as it's cracked up to be. If your problem is actually a foul odor in a small confined space, consider Frasier Fir spray by a company named Thymes. A short burst and it smells like you are sitting in the woods.

—Keep Smilin'. Dr. R.V. Shrink

Camped along the Rio Grande enjoying a nice hot spring soak

RV community

Dear Dr. R.V. Shrink:

I want to start living on the road for extended periods of time but my wife is afraid she will give up community. She likes our social life and is afraid she will not know anyone if we are moving all the time. We spend the winter in three different RV parks and have many friends. I am trying to convince her we will meet people in a travel mode, but she says it won't be the same. Can you shed some light on this subject, so we can expand our horizons?

—Community Centered in Carbondale

Dear CCC:

Community comes in all forms. It sounds like you two are very outgoing, so finding friends will be no problem whatever you decide to do. A community does not have to be local, such as an RV park or home and city. As you are out doing things you enjoy, you will meet people who like the same things. You can connect with these same people year after year. With all the social media available today it is so easy to keep in touch with people you meet on the road. You will make life-long friends while doing something as simple as a ranger walk. Every time you move to a different location you will end up with new neighbors. You will have ample opportunity to meet like-minded people whatever mode of travel you choose. My advice is to expand your base and raise your peak. The world is your oyster and you will find it full of pearls if you open yourself to meeting new friends as you travel. The only downside could turn out to be your wife not wanting to ever come home again.

—Keep Smilin', Dr. R.V. Shrink

RV singing telegram

Dear Dr. R.V. Shrink:

I love living in our small, secure, warm and dry space. Sometimes I feel like we live in a space capsule. We find these incredible places to park. The weather can turn sour, yet we are still warm and happy in our 5th wheel home. This might sound petty, but it is driving me nuts. My problem is noise pollution. It doesn't bother my husband, but I can't take it any longer. Because of our small square footage, I can't escape the annoying sound coming from our water heater. It is a high pitch, constant squeal. My husband insists it is normal because the water heater still works fine. But I never heard this before. It only does it when we have electric hook-ups. Am I being too fussy? Is this something I should try to block from my mind? Is it a sign that something is about to happen? Should I sing in a high pitch to my husband to demonstrate how annoying I find it?
—Sounding Board in Bozeman

Dear Boze:

Singing to your husband will just complicate a very simple situation. It should never come down to solving annoyance with annoyance. What you have is a failing heat element. It could be solved by flushing the tank and cleaning the element, but if you are going to the trouble of pulling the element, you might just as well replace it for twenty bucks. It really doesn't make any more noise than when you are heating with gas, but I agree the pitch could drive you nuts. I would explain to your husband that he will be dealing with the problem sooner or later. There is no time like the present. Your husband is in hot water right now, but the singing telegram you are getting is a sign you will soon be changing your tune to the "Sound of Silence." I can't remember all the lyrics, but it goes something like this, "Hello darkness, my old friend, there's no hot water once again..." It is a good idea to flush the tank at least once a year. If you have a tank that is not aluminum you might want to consider adding an anode rod to help prevent future buildup on the heating element.

—Keep Smilin', Dr. R.V. Shrink

Enlightenment

RV go si'

Dear Dr. R.V. Shrink:

I know it is only June, but I am in a heated discussion with my wife about where we are headed this coming winter. We have tried all the supposedly warm southern destinations in the U.S. and are often holed up in the motorhome because it is too cold outside. The problem is, I want to go as far down the Baja Peninsula as possible and spend the winter where I am guaranteed warmth. My wife watches too much news and thinks everyone that goes to Mexico is in grave danger. I am not ignorant of the facts, I just know that a lot of RVer's go into Mexico every winter and seem to have no problem. Am I asking too much? Do you think I would be putting my wife under too much pressure?

—Baja in a Bounder from Boise

Dear Bounder:

Before you go, I think you should both be comfortable with it. Having your wife spend the winter out of her comfort zone would defeat the whole purpose of living the RV dream. It will take some studying on your part. You'll want to make sure you know the rules and regulations of entering and traveling into

Mexico. Carry the right insurance, have your passports, and take no weapons. That is just the beginning of what you should be aware of. My suggestion would be for you to read and study the many up-to-date forums and blogs of RVer's who do this every winter. I would share this information, good and bad, with your wife as you progress. Knowing that thousands of others are doing the same thing might make her begin to feel more comfortable about the adventure. Many people who RV to Mexico will tell you they have never had a problem. This might very well be true. However, if you read the U.S. Embassy Report online, you will find it's not true for everyone that travels there. You might want to find others to caravan with. Safety in numbers can be a much less stressful way to travel into Mexico. Most people find services very accommodating in Mexico, some say more accommodating than many of the snowbird areas of the U.S. The bottom line: There is a lot of insanity in the beautiful areas just south of our borders. Caution is advised, but with the right preparations, you are most likely not to have any problems. Traveling close to the border in the U.S. can have its own dangers, but you will find a heavy law enforcement presence and the insurance that they are there to help you. It's not like the old western films in Mexico where the good guys wear the white hats and the bad guys wear the black hats. It's a personal choice. My only suggestion is that you are both comfortable with the decision before going.

—Keep Smilin', Dr. R.V. Shrink

RV carpet concern

Dear Dr. R.V. Shrink:

My husband thinks I am stuck in a groove. He says I keep playing the same song over and over. The problem is I want to be a carpetbagger. I don't know why RV manufacturers even put carpeting in rigs. Carpet starts out looking nice, but quickly becomes soiled, path worn and matted. I want to rip ours out and replace it with tile or linoleum. My husband continues to resist the idea. He thinks it would make the trailer look bare and less warm. He also contends that it might have some function to play with the slides since it is only carpeted where the slide comes in. I think it is a catchall for dirt, hair and everything else that hits the floor. I am constantly sweeping handfuls of droppings from the tiled sections of our trailer, so I know that the carpet is just as dirty, holding onto this collection of debris in the fibers. The other problem is we seldom stay in parks with power. We have solar and love to find remote places to spend time. The only option we have for vacuuming is to fire up the generator and annoy everyone near us that came for the same reason we did, quiet and solitude. Should I just learn to live with this stuff? I am not a germaphobe, but I do like a clean trailer. We live in a small space and I want it spotless. I would appreciate any advice you could send my way.

—Not so magic carpet in Kalispell

Dear Kal:

If you are sounding like a broken record it is obvious you are not solving your disagreement in a satisfactory way. Manufacturers tend to offer what people want, what sells and what adds value to different models. I agree that a smooth surface is much easier to clean, but carpeting does have its plus sides. If removing it is not an option, you should start brainstorming about ways to deal with it that make it more desirable. A couple things come to mind immediately. There are many 12V hand vacs on the market that do a good job of sucking up carpet debris. Another option would be area rugs. Not only for the carpeted sections but also the smooth surface areas. They offer the advantage of removing and beating them outdoors. When they become too worn, or you tire of the design, it's a simple matter of replacing them with another throw rug. Because of the constant pounding, a carpeted area takes in a small space, you might want to consider raking the carpet before you vacuum. A small scrub brush works great for this. It yields a lot of hair and loosened debris you would otherwise miss. Having the carpet completely removed and replaced with tile is very doable. You would have to check with your manufacturer on your slide system. There may be some consideration as to how it rides in areas you want to redesign. Don't sweep your disagreements under the rug. Get them out in the open and make some decisions that both of you can live with. If you don't get your way this time, you will just have to "suck it up." Sorry, I couldn't resist. You might want to read Richard Carlson's book: "Don't sweat the small stuff. And it's all small stuff."

—Keep Smilin'. Dr. R.V. Shrink

City of Rocks campsite near Silver City, New Mexico

Pedal paddle or battle

Dear Dr. R.V. Shrink:

We live full-time on the road with no garage. We have a mid-sized motorhome and pull a small car. I love to pedal and my wife loves to paddle. The problem is I don't think we can carry both bikes and boats. She wants me to store kayaks on the motorhome roof, but I think that is inconvenient, dangerous, and a nightmare waiting to happen every time I need to get them down. How do you think we should solve this issue? Taking one of each is not an option.

—Toyless hauler in Harrisburg

Dear Toyless:

Many people go through this same process when first starting out in the RV lifestyle. Where there is a will, there is a way. The process should begin before you even choose a rig. Thinking ahead as to what equipment you may need to bring along and how to organize it is very important. In this situation I can think of several solutions you may consider besides arguing. Inflatable kayaks would be easy to fit into a storage bay or car trunk. Hard-sided kayaks could be racked on the car roof. I have even seen racks that fit kayaks vertically on the rear of motorhomes. Same with bikes. Rack them on the car or the rear of the motorhome. If you use the car for hauling, you will often want to off-load when stopping for some length of time and slide the boats under the motorhome. Having a bike rack for just the motorhome can be a problem when you want to transport them to a trailhead. Having the capability to transport both with your tow car will be convenient in many situations. I have seen people hauling everything you can imagine. There are all kinds of racking systems. You are working on a common combination with many workable solutions. They even have kayaks with pedals. Check out Hobie Cat kayaks. Good luck.

—Keep Smilin', Dr. R.V. Shrink

I don't do RV windows

Dear Dr. R.V. Shrink:

We laughed out loud when we read your column about the guy constantly working on his rig. My husband is just the opposite.

When he retired he thought it meant he never had to lift a finger again unless it was to push a button on his remote. To keep him from becoming a total couch potato I do encourage him to work on a few honey-do jobs occasionally. Recently he cleaned all the windows on the fifth-wheel. We are spending a month in Colorado and have a mountain view out our picture window that should be on a calendar. It looked great in the full sun but at sunset, we could see all the water spots and streaks as if he had never cleaned them. He thinks his time was totally wasted and never wants to work on a window again. I am not looking through spotty windows for the rest of my life. It is causing some friction to say the least. Am I asking too much? Is an RV any different than a house? Does everyone with an RV have to look through stained glass?

—Glass Half Dirty in Durango

Dear Dirty:

It can be frustrating when you spend the time to do a job and it comes out looking bad. Cleaning methods can differ from a stationary home to a home on wheels. RV owners are always battling road grime. Your husband did not waste his time. He probably removed the worst layer of dirt and is now down to the tough marks from hard water. If you check the internet you will find dozens of window cleaning methods that all work to some extent. In my humble opinion, the best method is steel wool. You need to purchase a package of "four aught" steel wool. Four zero's on the package. This will not scratch your glass unless it has some type of coating. Do a small area to experiment, but in most cases, there will be no problem. Steel wool (0000) will take off bugs, road tar, hard water spots, and sap. When you're done with that use any kind of window cleaner to finish up. Once your husband finds out how easy this method is, and how well it works, he may go into the RV mobile window cleaning business. He may discover those mountains outside your clean windows and watch something besides TV. When you need the windows cleaned in the future, you will say, "Where four aught thou." Then you will hear, "Thou is here on the couch."

—Keep Smilin', Dr. R.V. Shrink

Picnic at White Sands National Monument in New Mexico

RV venting

Dear Dr. R.V. Shrink:

We just let a dealer talk us into a vent cover for our automatic roof fan. It sounded like a great idea at first. When we leave for the day we like to leave the roof vent open and the fan on for our cat. It has a rain sensor, which is good and bad. It shuts when the weather turns wet, but then the cat gets less ventilation and that's not good on a hot day. We figured with the cover it could stay open rain or shine and give Fuzzbutt continuous ventilation. Now that we are five hundred miles down the road we find the vent doesn't open completely under the cover, airflow is significantly restricted and after a hard rain, the sensor still actuates the fan. My husband says, "Live and learn." I, on the other hand, want to call the dealer and give him an earful for misrepresenting the product to us. Am I just creating more stress for myself? Should I call it a bad investment and move on?

—Venting in Virginia City

Dear Venting:

You have learned a great new lesson. In the future, before you make a buying decision, do an online forum search. You will find dozens of people who have already made the purchase and posted their thoughts on the pros and cons of almost every product on the market. Perhaps the salesman was thinking less ventilation 100% of the time would be better than great ventilation part of the time. Most fans with all the bells and whistles have a manual mode. You should be able to bypass the rain sensor. If not you could easily remove it. If you decide you really can't live with the purchase, the dealer may offer you a return if you ask. If not, sell it on eBay, recoup some of your loss and move on. Sometimes it helps to give a product some time. It may work out better than you originally think. The cover should allow the fan lid to open the majority of the way, so the restriction you detect would be in the cover louvers. If it has a screen you may want to remove it since the fan is already screened into your interior. If you are upset and venting more than the fan cover, you could overheat and blow a gasket. It's not good for you, your husband or Fuzzbutt.

—Keep Smilin', Dr. R.V. Shrink

.

RV cleaning out the pipes

Dear Dr. R.V. Shrink:

I hate to sound paranoid, but recently we put cash in a Forest Service Campground fee pipe and it came up missing. A ranger came around to collect from us and we showed him our receipt. He said there was no matching envelope in the pipe. After convincing him that we had paid, he took our word and honored our receipt. Now every time I put money in one of those seemingly secure fee pipes I worry about it. Do you think I am being silly? We do this all the time and my husband says, "Get over it!"

—Nervous Nellie in Nevada

Dear Nellie:

Believe it or not, crooks with low aspirations have learned to fish envelopes from fee pipes. If you talk to a few host volunteers you will hear stories of string and gum, coat hanger fishing and super glue tangling. Fee pipe security is really not your problem. Pay your fee, keep your receipt and leave crime solving to management. I am sure the ranger who talked with you has dealt with this problem in the past and will again in the future. When dropping cash, check or charge card info into those pipes, you now know they could end up in the wrong hands. If it would help you sleep better, try using checks. Most low-level crooks, trying to support a meth habit, won't deal in checks, they want hard cash. But for security reasons, cash is probably your safest bet. Pipe heists are probably very uncommon, but caution is advised. We always look the fee pipe over very carefully. Fake fee pipes have been used by crafty crooks. We also eyeball gas pumps for card readers that have been placed in the credit card slot to steal information. Having your card info ripped off is much more of a problem. It happened to us in North Central Florida this winter. By the time we figured it out, the bad guys had pumped three hundred bucks worth of gas, Simonized their vehicle, ate at McDonald's and then celebrated with a stop at a liquor store. The card company removed the charges from our account, but we were without a credit card for a while until they issued us a new one. There is a difference between paranoid and cautious. Two out of every five people suffer from paranoia. The other three are watching them suspiciously.

—Keep Smilin', Dr. R.V. Shrink

Double teaming the dirty swirly job—Takes just minutes when done properly

RV Tow Row

Dear Dr. R.V. Shrink:

We bought a motorhome we love. My wife and I studied many RVs, how we would use one, where we would take one, and what type of floor plan we desired. That process went very smoothly. Now we are trying to figure out what type of tow vehicle to purchase and are currently at polar-opposite ends of the scale on what we need, what we can afford, and how we will use it. We are not looking for any brand information — we just want some clue as to what we should be considering so that we can both back off our demands and find some middle ground.

—Tow to Tow in Tampa

Dear Tampa:

It sounds like you two are very methodical in your approach to making a purchase. It's refreshing to hear you are both actively engaged in making decisions together. These are large investments that will affect both of you for many years. Getting it right the first time is not as common as you might think. With little information as to what your needs and wants are in a toad, let me just give you some food for thought. In the end, you will have to make the final decision on your own. There are all kinds of contraptions for pulling a vehicle behind a motorhome, protecting it from stone damage, and keeping it within safety regulations. If you like to explore back roads, you might want to consider high clearance and four-wheel drive. If you are looking for extra storage, shop a small to mid-sized pickup. If you are hauling bikes or kayaks on the vehicle, think about rack space and fit. Consider weight and towing capacity and how it will affect your fuel mileage. Even a light vehicle will most likely cost you a mile per gallon. New or used? No matter what you do to protect a toad, expect stone damage, tar and road grime maintenance, and some additional tire wear from towing sway. If you observe the many other RVers pulling a vehicle behind a motorhome you will see a wide variety of choices. Some will need more accessories than others. The additional expense can include brakes, transmission pumps, dollies, lights, and wiring. Personally, I continue to buy old Saturn SL's on Craigslist. Unfortunately, they aren't making them any longer. They were too reliable and economical. They are also under 2500 lbs. and easy to dingy-tow four wheels down. Our decision is based on easy to fix, easy to connect and disconnect and, because of the weight, fuel efficient while towing. Also, I don't have to take it to Best Buy or the Apple Genius Bar to get it fixed. List all your needs and wants. Once you agree on those, there are many vehicles to choose from today.

—Keep Smilin', Dr. R.V. Shrink

Hail to the Chieftain

Dear Dr. R. V. Shrink:

We are heading north after our first winter in Arizona. We imagined everything about our first year of retirement and looked forward to spending it exploring the Southwest. What we didn't imagine was the risk of getting home in the spring. We ran smack into a weather pattern that dropped golf ball size hail on our new rig. It looks like it has been pelted with cue balls. I thought we were heading home too soon, but my husband was chomping at the bit to get started. What I thought would be a relaxing trip north has turned out to be a nightmare. Is this a regular occurrence? Is severe spring weather something we should learn to deal with? I am not playing the blame game, but I think we should stay south longer and avoid the transition storms we have dealt with this year. My husband thinks it was just bum luck. Any thoughts?

—Hail Mary in Minnesota

Dear Mary:

Heading north in the spring with flocks of other migrating snowbirds can get dicey. No one seems to be able to predict the weather, but forecast science gets better all the time. It would be wise to invest some time in the weather channel, weather apps, maybe even a weather radio. The more information the better. You may want to plan a route that skirts geography that is notorious for the worst spring weather outbreaks of tornadoes, hail, wind, and flooding. After a lot of homework, you can still experience bum luck and just be in the wrong place at the wrong time. When that happens, find a safe harbor for your land yacht and park it until it looks safe to be out on the road again. Hail can be very damaging to metal, glass, and paint. It is all repairable after negotiating with your insurance company. Following spring home can often be as enjoyable as the whole winter of travel. Try not to let this experience ruin numerous years of future, trouble-free travel.

—Keep Smilin', Dr. R.V. Shrink

Discovering how it all began at the RV Hall of Fame museum in Elkhart, Indiana

RV water boy

Dear Dr. R.V. Shrink:

I can lead my wife to water, but I can't make her drink. We travel in our fifth wheel several months a year. We are usually in the West in the summer and Florida in the winter months. My wife will not drink the water we put in our tanks. I have filters on the inlet, filters at the sink, and pitcher filters strictly for drinking water. She has a hang-up about where we get some of our water, often near dump stations. In Florida she says it smells like sulfur and tastes like swamp water; out in New Mexico, she read about a leaky waste site with groundwater contamination from the Hiroshima bomb. I can't win. She would keep buying bottled water even if I hooked up to a sparkling glacier. Don't you think this borders on paranoia? I don't think many RVers are dying from drinking water. Please let me hear from you on this issue.

—Water Boy in Boynton

Dear Water Boy:

I would not call this paranoia. Paranoia would be anxiety or fear based on irrationality and delusion. Your wife has some very real concerns. I'm not sure buying bottled water is the answer — who knows where that came from. Actually, you might not want to bring that point up. Some Florida water does contain sulfur. It is wise to flush your tanks after spending a winter down there, especially your hot water tank. As for New Mexico, she has a right to be concerned. The waste from our first bomb experiments is leaking into the Rio Grande. It is also causing some concern near Carlsbad, where some of it was moved and stored. Most dump stations are signed to show "potable" and "non-potable" water. However, if you do enough traveling you will see people using the wrong hose for the wrong purpose. I have tried to educate many foreign visitors with rented motorhomes as to which hose is for sewer rinse and which is for filling the fresh water tank. Some people are more susceptible to waterborne disease than others. I have been drinking unfiltered water in the backcountry for fifty years without incident. My wife thinks I am going to die from giardia. So far so good. I think you should continue taking every precaution that makes your wife feel comfortable. Nothing is going to be foolproof, but good sanitation habits, concern over your water sources, and good old common sense should keep you safe wherever you travel.

—Keep Smilin', Dr. R.V. Shrink

Stop in the name of love before you "brake" my heart

Dear Dr. R.V. Shrink:

I love to stop at thrift shops and antique stores when we travel. The problem is my husband always has some reason not to stop. Usually, it is because he doesn't see adequate parking for our motorhome and tow car, too much traffic, or not enough time to look over the parking situation before we pull in. I seldom drive so I can't argue those facts. I am wondering if it is just my husband, or do other RV drivers have the same problem parking spontaneously when they see a place they would like to stop along the way. I don't want to miss half of America just because of parking restrictions for our size. This has caused several arguments already. Please give me some advice.

—Denied Access in Arizona

Dear Denied:

There are some trade-offs for having a large, luxurious home on wheels. Many stores, attractions and even fuel stops have limited space for parking or pull-throughs. Depending on your size, spontaneity can often go out the window. You do not want to be indecisive when making a turn into an area you are not familiar with. If you are not sure what you are doing, you can be sure the traffic behind you has no clue. In your case, my suggestion would be to look for the nearest suitable parking area you can find, drop your tow vehicle from the Mother Ship, and go back to businesses that look too tight to maneuver into blindly. Many people learn this lesson the hard way. I, like many people, would be guilty as charged. I can recall several times having to unhook the toad and work my way out of a tight situation. I once had a guy in the Florida Keys yelling at me. He was upset because he had just lost a bet. He had bet his friend fifty dollars that I would never get turned around and out of the parking lot. Those pulling a 5th wheel or trailer do not have the luxury of unhooking. You can't always plan ahead. I understand that many interesting stops just appear unannounced. That is one of the great things about RV travel. That said, you still need to be realistic as to your capabilities, skills, options, and nerves, when making a split-second decision to sail into uncharted waters. My wife and I just watched a couple completely destroy a brand new fifth-wheel. They pulled into a narrow, state park campground loop. Instead of stopping and assessing the situation, they panicked. Before we could get to them they tore up both sides of the rig, ripped the ladder off, and dented the storage doors under the front hitch. You might want to drive more often. It will give you a fresh perspective on how your husband is thinking. It will also give you some confidence and skills you might one day need if something were to happen to him.

—Keep Smilin', Dr. R.V. Shrink

Peaceful morning reflections camped along the shore of
Montana's Pray Lake

RV work in progress

Dear R.V. Shrink:

We are now living full-time in our motorhome. To convince
me this was a good idea my husband argued that we would not
have all the house maintenance chores that used to eat up so much
of our time. As it turns out, he is still constantly working on our
motorhome and tow car. He has just become a slave to a new
possession. I'm not sure if we own the motorhome or it owns us.
There always seems to be something he has to tighten up, button
down, add, drain or clean. Is this normal? I sometimes think he is

obsessed with working on our new home on wheels.

—Worn out from watching in Wenatchee

Dear Wenatchee:

It's called precautionary maintenance. It is a necessary evil whether you own a home, a boat, or an RV. Part of the problem with full-time RV living is not having a convenient place to work on some projects that need to be done. Most parks do not allow mechanical work to be performed on site. Many won't even allow you to wash your rig. Keeping things lubed, cleaned, tightened and in good working order, will save you time and money in the long run. Everyone has a different skill level when it comes to keeping their RV in tiptop shape. But regardless, these things have to be done sooner or later. It sounds to me like your husband is on top of things. You should be grateful he is so diligent about it. We have a home base. We make a pit stop once a year and do all the major maintenance that is harder to do on the road with fewer tools and less opportunity to find an allowable space to work on projects. Most precautionary maintenance chores take little time if you stay on top of them. Your husband probably enjoys this work and has some pride in ownership. Those are great traits.

—Keep Smilin', Dr. R.V. Shrink

RV toxic cloud

Dear Dr. R.V. Shrink:

We just started RVing this winter. We are in our fourth month. RV life is now shifting from the imagined to the realistic state. It is not as placid as I had imagined, but still very enjoyable. We are still learning about where we like to explore, the need for reservations in some areas, what types of parks we like, and the days we like to move or sit. Everything is falling into place and we are beginning to feel like we are now part of the lifestyle and not still in boot camp. I have to say, one of my first real shocks was a situation you brushed on a couple weeks ago. We were sitting out under our awning having breakfast. It was a beautiful warm morning. The birds were singing, the sun was rising, and you could almost hear the flowers growing. Just through the palmetto hedge, we could see the neighbor packing up for departure. All of a sudden our tranquil morning turned into a nightmare of stink. Even knowing we were sitting there, the guy dumped his sewer without so much as a by-your-leave. I almost gagged before I got inside our rig. I know dealing with waste holding tanks is a necessity, but isn't there some code of conduct that should go along with the procedure?

—Smelly Nelly in Naples

Dear Nelly:

I would agree that if the person saw you sitting out and did not give you some warning, that was rude. I believe you will find this is a rare case the more you travel. There is no question you will end up dealing with individuals with all kinds of idiosyncrasies. The RV lifestyle is no different than life in general. You will run into those people that just don't think their blackwater stinks. They say, "Timing is everything." I think you will find that most people will be a bit more stealth when they dump their tanks in close quarters. Let's give this person the benefit of the doubt and assume he is newer at this than you are. Perhaps he didn't realize he was going to release a toxic cloud of stink into your site.

Continue to enjoy your travels. I can guarantee you will find nine friendly and courteous camping site neighbors for every annoying one you encounter.

—Keep Smilin', Dr. R.V. Shrink

Instruction

RV campsite property rights

Dear Dr. R.V. Shrink:

We were parking overnight at a casino in Las Vegas with a group of friends. We were all headed across the parking area where other RVs were parked when a man came out of his trailer and said we were trespassing on his property. At first, we thought he was kidding, but as it turned out he was very serious. Obviously, in his mind, this patch of the casino parking lot was his property and we were trespassing. On our way back he came out to talk to us as if the first confrontation never took place. This frightened me, but everyone else just laughed it off. I was a bit nervous the rest of the night. Do you think I am being silly? This is not normal behavior and I think living for a short period just feet from someone with a Jekyll and Hyde personality is a bit disconcerting.

—Nervous in Nevada

Dear Nevada:

There is nothing wrong with being cautious in all traveling situations. It is not uncommon to run into people with issues, especially in free camping areas. There are many people living on the fringe, many in RVs, that suffer from psychiatric disorders, substance abuse, and various addictions. I think in most cases the right approach would be courtesy, compassion, and caution. Everyone has their own threshold for patience and comfort levels in these types of encounters. If you find you are not comfortable then don't encourage conversation, keep interactions at a minimum, or simply move on. To paraphrase John Bradford, "There, but for the grace of God, go I." That said, you still have to determine for yourself what is provocation and what is annoyance. If you feel threatened, move on. During a normal year on the road, camping in all types of areas, remote and urban, we have encountered a situation similar to this just a few times. Seldom are we forced to share a site with another camper, but recently at a Corps of Engineers park in Florida we could only book a combined site. As it turned out, we shared this site with a guy living in his van. I went over, shook his hand and introduced myself as his new neighbor. He seemed as normal as me, which should have been my first clue. Soon we noticed he was talking loud to someone in a very angry voice. At first, we thought he must have an ear-bud phone and he was arguing on the phone with someone. Soon we realized he was talking to himself about us. He was very polite when we talked to him, but the voice in his head was not happy sharing a site with us. As it turned out the voice won and he moved on, but first, he knocked on our door and asked if we needed anything at the store. He was going into town shopping and would be glad to pick up whatever we needed. When I told him we were all set, he started rattling off items he thought we might need...steaks, beer... I'm not sure if he or the voice wanted our money. Then he never returned. When I talk about caution, it is not only these types of situations you have to be concerned with. RVing or not, there are people out there that want to scam you and I'm not just talking about your cell provider and your insurance company. This winter at a Yuma,

AZ casino, RVers were scammed in a "Three Card Monte" game set up by men in the free parking area. Your odds are bad enough if you go inside, why play in the parking lot! Ninety percent of the time, free casino parking is only free if you "DON'T" go inside. If you do, you had better read the Wizard of Odds, so you know which of the sucker games are going to drain your pockets the most efficiently. Let common sense be your guide and you should be just fine.

 —Keep Smilin', Dr. R.V. Shrink

.

RV listing

Dear Dr. R.V. Shrink:

 My husband is a real gadget guy. He is always reinventing the wheel when it comes to our trailer. Before our last trip, he direct-wired a small inverter to our coach batteries with heavy wire. It has been great for charging our computers, phones, and cameras. The inverter sits in a small basket on the dinette seat. We came home one day and our trailer was full of smoke. I had left some notepads and coupons in the basket and the inverter was hot enough to ignite them. Why it didn't burn the whole place down, I don't know. I think we should remove the whole thing, but my husband said it was a fluke and that the system is perfectly safe as long as we keep things clear of it. For peace of mind shouldn't we just scrap the whole thing? Is it worth the worry? I don't want to be unreasonable, but this could have been a real disaster.

 —Giving up smoking in Sedona

Dear Sedona:

If wired properly the inverter should be as safe as any other electrical system in your trailer. I would lose the basket and mount it so that you won't pile anything on top of it. One thing you should consider is a "LIST." I have talked about lists before. Many people have a checklist for departure — making sure everything is unhooked, turned off and put away properly. Another checklist can be used when leaving your rig for the day, or a few hours. Check things like stove burners, electrical items, Wi-Fi, water, awning, even making sure the cat is in sight. It's easy to forget things and some can become damaging and even disastrous. Many lessons come from experiences. "What does not kill us, makes us stronger." We always turn the water off outside when leaving for the day. We learned this the wet way. Our daughter's loom, stored in the shower, fell against the cold water knob. We left for the day and fortunately, the park owner turned the water off when she saw it pouring from beneath the motorhome. Everything was a soggy mess, but it could have been worse. What if the toilet malfunctioned? There would have to be a sequel to the Robin Williams RV movie. Since we started a daily departure checklist we have found the cat shut in the closet, the burner left on low from morning breakfast, Wi-Fi hotspot left on, vents opened, and awning up. Making a list and checking it twice will ease your mind and save you from dealing with many issues.

—Keep Smilin', Dr. R.V. Shrink

RV birdwatching in the desert Southwest

Ralph Kramden an RV

Dear Dr. R.V. Shrink:

I have been wanting to write to you, I just had to wait until I was pushed over the psychological edge. We stay in many campgrounds that are tighter than a wax doll's eardrum. This week we were in a campground that was so tight my truck mirrors were almost touching my neighbor's. The real problem is, I like to get on the road early in the morning when we travel. My wife, however, will not let me make any noise until the neighbors are up and moving around. She thinks we will annoy people if we bring our slides in, lift our jacks, start the engine, or even unhook the utilities. Wouldn't this come under the heading of, "That's life in the tight lane?" Can I buy a silencer that will fit on my Ford diesel? Am I being unreasonable? I seem to be the only one restricted. Everyone else leaves at dark-thirty and doesn't seem to be concerned that I'm sleeping. My wife says, "If they jump off a cliff, it doesn't mean you have to jump off a cliff." I'm getting to the point that I DO want to jump off a cliff. Please stop me.

   —Ralph Kramd-en in Kissimmee

Dear Kramd-en:

   Unfortunately, the "highest and best use for real estate theory" seems to prevail for commercial park owners. It's all about how many units they can squeeze into a given parcel of ground. Some are much worse than others. The noise you make, coming and going, should always be a concern, but I believe most RVer's understand that fellow travelers often leave early and that it is something we all deal with. Staying in parks with tight quarters comes with many drawbacks, but you know all of them going in. Sometimes you sit out on your patio with a gorgeous view of the ocean or desert and sometimes you sit out on the patio with a not-so-gorgeous view of your neighbor's sewer connection. Jumping off a cliff is not the solution. Florida's highest elevation is under 350 feet and I don't think it's a cliff. In fact, you might be eaten by an alligator just getting there. My suggestion would be to pack up, as much as possible, the night before, and make a courtesy call at the neighbors and let them know you will be leaving early. Some people complain if they are hung with a new rope, but at least you have made the effort to warn them, which shows you are concerned about your possible annoyance. Crowded campgrounds are a way of the RV lifestyle. I'm waiting to see campground owners going up a few stories with RV campground parking garages. I have already seen airplane hanger type structures in North Dakota to house RV oilfield workers during the subzero winters and hot summers. Know that noise pollution is a part of living in a high-density campground, and that everyone is well aware of it.

—Keep Smilin', Dr. R.V. Shrink

Belting my RV husband

Dear Dr. R.V. Shrink: We just started traveling in a Class A motorhome. I am so glad my husband talked me into bumping up from our Class C. I have this gigantic windshield of the world in front of me, as America unfolds before my eyes. We sit up so much higher and with the large side windows it almost seems we are in a fishbowl looking out. My only complaint is I have to always nag my husband to wear his seatbelt. I am constantly telling him, "Click It, or Ticket." He thinks he is at home in his La-Z-Boy. How can I impress on him that wearing his belt is not only a good idea but a safety measure that everyone should follow?

—Tightening my belt in Anza-Borrego

Dear Anza:

It's simple. Refuse to ride with him. He is not only endangering himself but you and every other motorist you come across. Just because you are one of the bigger vehicles on the road does not make you immune to catastrophe. Have him Google Images "motorhome accidents." Maybe the shock value will help convince him. If things go "south" one day, it will happen in a flash. He especially should be belted in because he is manning the helm. He will be in a much better position to control the motorhome if he is still in his seat, not up on the dash with his face pushed up against the windshield. Even without another vehicle involved, simply going off the shoulder can be a disaster if you are not belted in and do not study your driving options ahead of time. Know what to do, and not to do, when you drop off the shoulder, blow a tire, or encounter a moose. The first and most important advantage in all these scenarios is having your seatbelt on. You could give him some old commercial advice. "It's not only a good idea, it's the LAW!" You could also drive him nuts singing the old seat belt jingle over and over. Here are the words if you have forgotten. Buckle up for safety, buckle up. Buckle up for safety, always buckle up. Show the world you care, use it everywhere. Buckle up for safety. When you're driving Buckle Up! Maybe you simply change your vocabulary too, " Click it or Stick it.

—Keep Smilin', Dr. R.V. Shrink

Dog sitting for camping neighbors who wanted to go day hiking

RV lifestyle voodoo economics

Dear Dr. R.V. Shrink:

We just stayed for one night at a Louisiana State Park. We went in without a reservation. Dry camping was $14 per night. When I looked at my credit card receipt I noticed I was charged $20. My receipt said the $6 was a reservation fee. When I questioned it I was told everyone is charged $6 the first night to pay for the Reserve America system they use for keeping track of their state campgrounds. I have never heard of this before. There is nothing on their park websites that explain this in advance. The park attendant never explained it when I paid, and she was even a bit huffy when I questioned it. Have you ever heard of this before? Am I the only one that thinks this is a bit strange? My wife says, "Get over it!" Should I?

—Nailed in New Orleans

Dear Nailed:

Your wife is right, get over it. Does it make sense? Not really. I questioned it as much as you did the first time I experienced it. To be honest I took it a few steps further. I was so curious I called the Louisiana State Park office and asked for more of an explanation. I was told they have tried running their own software and found it much more expensive than paying Reserve America six bucks for every paid camper night in their parks annually. What they couldn't tell me is what that number is. They have 22 State Parks and everyone pays, reservation or not. What I found most unusual was that they had no reference to this charge on their website or their Fees and Facilities Guide. When I questioned this, I was told I just missed it. I asked to be directed to where it is on their site. What I found was a reservation fee for six bucks. It states nowhere that everyone is charged this fee. Strange but true. That said, Louisiana is priced fairly and competitively when compared to other states. Every state seems to have a different management vision. Texas, for example, charges 7 bucks per person per night for an entrance fee on top of camping. If you do not have an annual pass, you pay this fee every night. A couple would have to stay in Texas State Parks at least five times a year to break even on the annual pass. If you are just passing through it is often not the most economical camping. Other states tax campground fees, which add up quickly. Louisiana does recognize seniors with half-priced camping. This is good for not only Louisiana residents, but any state that honors the senior passport the same as Louisiana. Unfortunately, that is only Arkansas, Delaware, and Maryland. It takes some time to become familiar with all the various state and federal campground fees, rules and regulations. To the mix, you can now add concessioners. They seem to be taking control of public lands. I still have a hard time grasping the voodoo economics of public tax dollars subsidizing corporate managed state, federal and national park campgrounds, run by volunteers. In Louisiana, it seems state government can't manage a website and the Federal Government is finding it harder all the time to manage a simple campground. A government bean counter recently figured out that the legacy costs of Smokey the Bear could be enormous because bears are now living much longer. If Smokey retires and refuses to take a buyout his pension costs could become a fiscal anchor on the Forest Service. Smokey the Bear could soon be put on the endangered species list, replaced by a volunteer in a Yogi suit.

—Keep Smilin', Dr. R.V. Shrink

RV sail

Dear Dr. R.V. Shrink:

My wife is mad, I'm sad, the dog is glad. Let me explain. We had the dog tied to the awning support. My wife walked several sites over to talk to another couple. It was a breezy morning and the awning was making some noise, but nothing too serious. Before my wife left she said we should roll it up, but I pooh-poohed the idea saying, "It's fine!" Well, we must have had a microburst of wind, because we heard the dog yelp, metal crinkle, plastic crack and neighbors screaming. In the blink of an eye, the awning blew over the motorhome. It snapped the dog leash, broke the TV antenna, cracked two ceiling vent covers, and trashed a thousand dollar awning. The dog was traumatized. He looked at me like, "I swear I didn't do a thing. I was just lying here sleeping!" I was conveying the same thing to my wife, but she wasn't buying it. I have been getting the hot tongue and cold shoulder ever since. Is it my fault? Shouldn't these things be engineered to take a wind blast? Should I have to roll it up every time I think there might be a wind event? My wife says we shouldn't even replace it. I think it comes in handy on occasion. Will this scare me for life? Will I always be gun-shy about deploying my awning? Please tell me there is therapy for a guy and his dog who were just trying to enjoy an afternoon siesta.

—Bob and Goober in "The Doghouse"

Dear Bob and Goober:

Bad things happen to good people and dogs. You have to let it go, move on, and learn from your experiences. You have learned some valuable lessons in this one event. First, always listen to your wife. Second, never second-guess an RV awning. Third, get a sturdier leash and a heavier dog. Seriously, you cannot fight Mother Nature. Physics teaches us just how powerful wind in a sail can be. Your RV awning is basically a horizontal sail. You can tie them down, stake them down, even hold them down, but the right wind will still rip them apart. Everyone has their own threshold of caution. I personally would not go to the store for an hour without putting the awning up. I have seen too many of them destroyed by just what you describe. The roll-up procedure takes about two minutes on a manual awning and thirty seconds on the new automatic models. No matter how careful you are, a micro-burst like you experienced can catch anyone off-guard. Your insurance should replace it. Maybe you can upgrade to the newest awning technology while you are at it. That way you, your wife and Goober can be trained on the newest awning operations. It helps when the chain of command can reach the lowest rank. With a new automatic awning, you should be able to blame it on Goober next time.

—Keep Smilin', Dr. R.V. Shrink

Talking RV under an apple tree can often solve any small problems you have

RVing can be a beach

Dear Dr. R.V. Shrink:

We are at Padre Island National Park in Texas. It is permissible to drive out on the beach and camp. I can see other large RVs out there, but my husband refuses to go. I even saw a big oil tanker truck drive down the beach for miles. My husband thinks we will sink in the sand, have the tide come in on us and get our rig all salty. I think it would be an experience that isn't possible in too many other locations. Do you think he is being over cautious, or am I being irresponsible insisting we try it?

—Wanting near the porpoise in Corpus

Dear Porpoise Corpus:

You are in an area where thousands of people drive for miles along the beach to fish, camp, beach-comb, go birding etc. There is a need to be cautious, but over-all it is perfectly safe if you use common sense. There are a few things to consider. If you do become stuck, a tow truck will be expensive. Once you are off the beach it would be a good idea to thoroughly wash down your rig. Treat it the same way you would an ocean-going fishing boat and motor. Even if you camp in the National Park campground up in the dunes, you will still get salty sand invading your rig when the wind blows. It is no different than driving south along hundreds of miles of salt covered roads. It needs to be cleaned and rinsed. You need to stay on the hard packed sand. You can see tire marks from other vehicles. There is plenty of wide areas to drive, turn around, park parallel, or back in and have your biggest picture windows facing the ocean. The Park Service visitor center can help you with tide information. A clue to leave would be waves washing under your rig. Rangers patrol the beach and will advise campers to leave if they see possible problems. As enchanting as the beach can be, it needs to be respected. You can enjoy wildlife right out your RV window, from coyotes to seabirds. Fantastic sunrises and great surf fishing are right out your door. You will save a few bucks because beach camping is free. If you can come to some kind of compromise, you might want to slowly get your feet wet (pun intended). You can camp right at the bottom of the road ramp down to the beach. You will be less than a hundred yards onto the beach and get the full effect of beach camping, the feel of the wheel on the hard packed sand, and experience the wave and wind action that you need to monitor. Walk the beach and talk to other campers. Most are more than happy to share their collective experience with you. The beach can look pristine one day and have the feel of a landfill the next, depending on weather and tide. But overall it is a wonderful place and beach camping can create wonderful memories if done properly.

—Keep Smilin', Dr. R.V. Shrink

RV power to the people, or not

Dear Dr. R.V. Shrink:

We invested in a whole solar array on our 5th wheel. We then invested in all new LED bulbs, 12v appliances and small inverters for charging our computers and cameras. With all this investment we seldom need or want electric service. In many cases, we are forced to pay for it anyway as many private, state and federal parks do not offer a choice of dry camping. In the good ole days you couldn't find hook-ups and now it is just the opposite. Are we just getting too old for our own good? We want simple and cheap, yet the RV industry is going complicated and expensive.

—Sunnyside up in Sedona

Dear Sunny:

Part of learning the RV lifestyle is understanding all the subtle nuances of finding what you are looking for. 1st, question everything. Many times things are not as they seem. For example, A park website may not offer dry camping when in reality it is available. You just have to ask. As more and more people are investing in solar, park managers realize there is a demand for sites not offering and charging for electricity. In many cases, management will give you a regular site and padlock the electric box. It can mean substantial savings. Many parks are now going to ala carte electric service. In that case, you have the option of using it or not. Many state parks have found an extra income stream in offering overflow camping instead of turning people away. This usually entails camping in a parking lot with no utilities. Being solarized can come in very handy when this situation arises. Depending on how you travel, a solar investment can pay for itself very quickly. The beauty of it is not having to give up any creature comforts if you are conservative with power usage. With enough mileage under your belt, you eventually understand the various management styles of various state-run parks. They all have different fee schedules, annual passes, senior discounts, etc. Many Federal parks are going to concessions and things change every year. You will find a treasure trove of information online and from fellow travelers but always check ahead of time with management for current information. When in doubt, ask. The worst thing that can happen is you will find you have no option in the matter. When it is cold or hot and you need heat or air conditioning, that A/C might look pretty good.

—Keep Smilin', Dr. R.V. Shrink

Camping in Florida's Big Cypress Swamp—Ten feet door to shore
with our very own gator

RV packrat

Dear Dr. R.V. Shrink:

Have you ever heard of rats that are afraid of light? My husband
seems to enjoy turning our RV into a light show. He started with
some Christmas lights this year and now is on to stringing the rig
with ribbons of LED lights. When I complained about not being
able to see the night sky because of light pollution emanating from
our motorhome, he said it was necessary to keep pack rats from
climbing up into our engine compartment at night and building

nests, chewing wires and pulling out insulation. I'm all for saving our engine from long-tailed vermin, but I don't think we need to turn a dark, quiet campground into Times Square. Am I being unreasonable? I can't help that I'm turned off by lights. I prefer the night sky.

—Shedding lights in Why

Dear Why:

Working out the kinks in a relationship is an ongoing challenge. Something new is always popping up, and you have to deal with it. In most cases, you can find some common ground. I would try to find that happy medium in this case. As for the pack rats, that is a very real threat. A couple of lights under the rig at night in packrat territory would be cheap insurance. They can cause expensive damage if they choose to move in with you. However, you would not need a light show. The LED strips are a great idea. They do not draw much juice and put out plenty of light. If you are in Why, Arizona, you might want to consider a small string of lights to run at night. You could wait until you both retire for the night and fire them up. Not so many that might annoy the neighbors, but just enough to annoy the pack rats. A couple cheap solar yard lights will also do the trick. Let the sun charge them all day, and throw them under the rig at night. If you are moving on a regular basis, it will most likely not be a problem. Staying put for a while might find your rig very inviting for several critters. If you end up going with the Broadway look, my suggestion would be to consider the neighbors.

—Keep Smilin', Dr. R.V. Shrink

Tiring RV

Dear Dr. R.V. Shrink:

We bought a used motorhome knowing we would have to do some updating on it. I am fairly handy and figured I could do most of the work myself. My biggest error was not calculating the price of new tires. Not ever having a vehicle that required truck-like tires, I had no idea they would be so expensive compared to car tires. It has made me a bit obsessive, according to my wife. I guess I am just trying to cut my losses as much as possible. I have been comparing prices with dealers, reading RV forums for hints on different brands, trolling for sales, and even thinking about seeing a psychic who might steer me (no pun intended) to a great deal on tires. The rig has Goodyear G670/70R19.5 F rated tires that I think are factory installed. They are 10 years old and I hate to start on a maiden voyage with these tired tire treads. I hope you can adjust my thinking so I don't feel so bad about emptying the bank account, or perhaps you have an uncle in the tire business. I would appreciate any help with tires or an attitude adjustment.

—Rubbernecking tire stores in Trenton

Dear Rubbernecking:

You are thinking correctly about a tire change. Ten years would be plenty on those treads, but not excessive. Dealers will tell you tires are like milk, they spoil. Most people only hear the first part of the advice and think tires will fall apart at 5 or 6 years. If cared for properly, inspected often, they can last much longer with proper alignment and rotation. If you buy new tires now, you can depreciate the cost over the next several years. Reading RV forums is a great idea, but you will find so many opinions about tires it will make your head spin. It's like asking for an opinion on who the best NFL team is. What you might want to concentrate on are warranty and accessibility. If you travel far and wide, buy a tire with a good warranty and a good network of dealers. Find a shop that not only sells tires but does alignment work. If you find a shop that is equipped to work on trucks and RVs you will find a much more experienced crew. Plan on spending five-hundred bucks a tire. You should be able to find a dealer that will get you out the door for that - tax, labor, and the whole nine yards. It is alright to be compulsive/obsessive. It is also fair to hit the tire manufacturer/dealer over the head with the spoiled milk theory. If tires become obsolete with age, you want the newest tires they can get their hands on. Those that say nothing, will end up with whatever comes off the shelf. You won't usually end up with tires that were made last week, but you don't have to take tires that are a year old already. Let them sell those to someone else. They may have to order a set from a distributor, but they can find newer date-stamped tires with a simple phone call and have them on the next delivery truck. Sorry, I don't have an uncle in the tire business. But if you talk to enough dealers you will find an average price for tire replacement in your area. Use online review sites to see what others have experienced with a dealer you may want to use. Online references can also help you discover whether the brand warranty is any good. See what others have experienced when they have had to scream, "Warranty!"

—Keep Smilin', Dr. R.V. Shrink

RVs come in all sizes, shapes and colors—Pick one and go

RV buying—Shop 'til you drop

Dear Dr. R.V. Shrink:

We have a dilemma that I am sure many people would love to have. We want to buy some type of RV and travel. The problem is, we have no clue what we want, need or should desire. We have gone from putting down a payment on a 32 ft. motorhome to seriously considering a 17 ft. travel trailer. We change our minds every day. Money is not the issue, even though some people might think we are cheap. It is not a problem of what my husband wants vs. what I want. We are both hopelessly confused. Please offer some counsel.

   —Dealing and not wheeling in West Virginia

Dear Virginia:
   There is a big difference between being cheap and being frugal. You are doing exactly what most people should do. Shop 'til you drop. So many people get over-excited with all the bells and whistles and buy the first thing they step into. Everyone has to find their own path. Having the financial wherewithal to pull the trigger on whatever you decide makes the decision making a bit easier. That said, RVs are an investment in a lifestyle, not the best ledger column if you are looking for appreciation on return monetarily. Now, let's try to tackle some of your doubts and needs. A lot of the decision making comes down to comfort. Comfort in driving, parking, and maneuvering. Comfort in living space, entertaining, and storage. Comfort in amenities. That can include everything from a bigger shower to satellite TV with 400 channels of bad programming. Not knowing what to expect and how you will travel leaves many options a dart-throw guess. That is the reason many people end up with two or more rigs before they figure out the perfect fit. Here are a few things you may not have figured into your buying decision so far: As last week's column stated, "weather happens." Often you are forced inside your rig for days when the weather turns sour. Don't buy something that will make you feel claustrophobic. One of the great things about RV travel is all the fantastic people you will meet. If you want

to invite them over for drinks, dinner or cards, will you have a comfortable space to accommodate entertaining? Most RVs are engineered to offer all the basic needs of a living space. They are "tiny houses." If you study enough floor plans you will begin to notice that they are all trying to accomplish the same thing. As you get longer and add slides, those spaces just give you more room in each compartment—bedroom, bathroom, kitchen, dining, living. As you get shorter and slideless, those compartments get smaller and often blended. This gives you the option to sleep in the dining room and cook in the bathroom. Do you want to drive a puller or a tower (toad) when you reach a destination? Have you figured out where to store the kayaks, ATVs, motorcycles, mountain bikes, fishing boat? Do you have a power plant and frame hefty enough to haul whatever load you plan to tote around? Do you have enough floor plan space to accommodate a business, hobby, craft or pet? Let me start to finish with advice I give everyone that ponders your questions. Talk to at least a dozen RVers, with a dozen different rigs. It will be the best investment in time you can make. You will get so much more honesty about the pros and cons from individuals than you will from commission-starved RV salespeople. Walk around campgrounds. You will see everything under the sun and find a lot of jovial people more than willing to tell you more than you probably want to hear. Take it all with a grain of salt. Glean from it the nuggets of information you may not have considered, and make your final decision. At that point, you could also rent one of the finalists in your RV beauty contest and try it out for a week. Remember, your final decision, may not be your final decision. If you go used, from an individual or a dealer, make sure everything on the unit is fired up and in working order.

—Keep Smilin', Dr. R.V. Shrink

RV ice shanty

Dear Dr. R.V. Shrink:

We headed for the warm sunny south the first part of November. We arrived in Florida and it was freezing. Since this is our first year traveling, we were a bit disillusioned. The only place on the map that looked warm was Arizona and Southern California. We made a hard right on I-10 and headed west. By the time we reached Deming, NM it was snowing. We have had the weather app out, scouring it for a warm place. None to be found unless we head for Southern Mexico. Is this what RV winter travel is all about? We could stay home wrapped in our blizzard blanket a lot cheaper than chasing the sun all over the country. Are we asking too much? Did we miscalculate? Should we sell this motorhome with a cracked frozen water pipe and look for a tent to rent in the Virgin Islands?

—Rolling Ice Shanty in Ajo

Dear Ajo:

You did miscalculate a bit. I think Mark Twain put it best, "Climate is what we expect, weather is what we get." My advice would be to slow down. I know gas is cheap right now, but as you have discovered, the jet stream can move faster than your motorhome. Stay south and let the warm weather find you. Don't drive thousands of miles looking for it. You can expect bouts of cold weather all over the south during the winter months. I understand why you had the misconception of warm sunny weather. You never see an advertisement of RVer's huddled inside their rigs trying to stay warm. More often you see them basking in the sun enjoying outdoor activity in shirt sleeves. The cold reality is "weather happens." When it does you have to deal with it, usually for short periods of time. Sorry to hear about your broken pipe. My suggestion would be to study your rig's plumbing and figure out what must be done during long nights of below freezing temps. Running your furnace heat through the duct system is better than just using an electric space heater in the coach. It helps to keep the basement storage area warm and protect it from freeze damage. If you have exposed holding tanks and pipes, consider heat tape. A light bulb in the plumbing compartment can often prevent a disaster by contributing just enough heat to keep things from freezing up. When you are feeling cold and despondent, turn on the weather channel and watch people commuting to work on the Dan Ryan in Chicago at 10 below. It will make you feel warm all over.

—Keep Smilin', Dr. R.V. Shrink

Direction

RV Border Patrol

Dear Dr. R.V. Shrink:

After reading your post about the birder woman wanting to go into remote areas all the time, I knew I had to write. My husband is very similar. He does not want to take the RV on poorly graded roads or even the car. He does, however, enjoy camping in wild places. I too do not care for crowds or commercial RV parks. We both enjoy hiking, paddling, and photography. Natural areas suit both of us. What I am not comfortable with are border areas in the Southwest. We recently spent some time at Buenos Aires Wildlife Refuge in Arizona. I protested a bit, but he convinced me that it was almost an armed camp with border patrol thicker than flies on the ground and in the air. The argument made sense, but we were parked alone in this vast grassland. When we stopped at the Visitor Center we met the volunteer hosts. I asked them where they camped. They were camped in a razor wire trimmed, chain linked fence compound near the headquarters. That should have been my first clue. We didn't have any problem, but I'm anxious all the time when we are in these areas. Is this just my hangup? Should I be more open-minded to exploring border areas?

—Anxious Annie in Arivaca

Dear Anxious:

I wouldn't suggest you do anything that makes you feel uncomfortable. Everyone has their own threshold when it comes to feeling secure while traveling. Many RVer's find special, remote sites that appeal to them for the very reasons you fear. Not to suggest there are no dangers in the area you are describing, but a few things should be considered. The first thing that comes to mind is the native population. Although sparse, many people live and work in that part of Arizona. You probably do not want to know everything that goes on in the area, but in most cases, it would not involve visitors to the refuge. You can't spend ten minutes along refuge roads without seeing Border Patrol and state and local police presence. Using common sense in where you travel and camp along the border will help ensure a safe experience. Traveling in numbers will also alleviate some of your apprehension. Remember that most of the pioneers traveled as a group and circled the wagons at night. The upside of the experience in this remote section of Arizona will be the wildlife and dark skies. It is a very unique grasslands area and you can expect to see pronghorn, burrowing owls, and masked bobwhite.

—Keep Smilin', Dr. R.V. Shrink

RV one butt kitchen

Dear Dr. R.V. Shrink:

We are first-time RVers. We sold our home in Tucson and just started traveling this winter in a 30 ft. motorhome. It gives new meaning to the term, "One Butt Kitchen." I enjoy cooking, but this minuscule space seems to crimp my style. The counter area and refrigerator/freezer are downsized enough to make normal cooking and storage a constant challenge. There is a definite order to getting things done with the least amount of difficulty! I am learning to approach meals in stages. So far I have said a few naughty words. My husband says I just have to adjust. Am I being unreasonable in comparing this closet cooking to the space I am accustomed?

—Super-downsized in Deming

Dear Down:

Learning to cope in an RV takes some adjustment. I would recommend starting out with some advice from W.C. Fields, "I cook with wine. Sometimes I even add it to the food." This should mellow you out a bit. On a more serious note, add some counter space. This is easily accomplished with a fold down counter extension, available at any RV store. If your stove doesn't already come with a cover, they can be purchased at Camping World or improvise with an upside down cookie sheet for added counter space. Refrigerator and freezer space often calls for shopping more often, but you will become accustomed to stocking the most important items in the space you have. The same applies to dry goods storage. Many RVer's have come up with collections of simpler meals that mimic what they have been used to cooking. You may try exploring downsized cooking utensils as well. Have you considered more outdoor cooking? There are a wide array of outdoor cooking appliances that will give you more options when weather permits. Much of your frustration is becoming familiar with your new space and developing a new routine. Speaking of a new routine, you might want to consider some advice from author Elizabeth Gilbert. She says, "A woman's place is in the kitchen...sitting in a comfortable chair, with her feet up, drinking a glass of wine and watching her husband cook dinner."

—Keep Smilin', Dr. R.V. Shrink

Make the Redwoods your RV backyard

RV tow truck

Dear Dr. R.V. Shrink:

I need your help. We bought a 34 ft. motorhome and my wife thinks we are on the Lewis and Clark Expedition. She is an avid bird watcher and is building her life list as we travel. We are now in the desert southwest and she has me driving down roads that I don't think are designed for a big motorhome. We don't know where half of them will lead. Often I have to unhook the tow car just so we can turn around. How can I convince her this is not a smart thing to do? I don't like conflict and it always turns into an argument, especially if there is a Mangrove Penguin to be found.

—Tow Truck Bound in Buckeye

Dear Towhee:

Sounds like a great adventure to me. However, I agree, you could get into trouble if you are not careful where you drive. I have several suggestions that might help and arguing is not one of them. First, download a free Google Earth App. The pictures are often a few years old, but unless you are studying a new road, it should be represented. Do a fly-over with Google Earth and see where the road leads. It will show you terrain, turnarounds, road conditions and much more. Another suggestion is to detach from the "Mothership" and go scout it out with your tow vehicle. It sounds like you should invest in a jeep if you haven't already. In the region of the country you are now exploring, there are multitudes of semi- backcountry camping sites that will accommodate a large RV. They happen to be in some of the best birding areas. Let me give you a suggestion. I am going to assume you are in Buckeye, Arizona. Go northwest a bit to Alamo Lake State Park. It has great birding with desert and riparian areas. Camp at the park for a night and explore all the BLM camping options around the park and the lake. Using both techniques I suggested above, you should be able to find a perfect site to bird, explore and hike, all inclusive with your free camping. The park offers sites with hookups or no hookups starting at fifteen bucks and they come with world-class sunrises and sunsets. You can also buy detailed maps of the areas you are exploring, but there is so much free information online, I would suggest you put it to use. Hiking across Arizona last spring I downloaded free topo maps of the whole state onto my GPS. These resources will not only tell you where you are but also tell you where to go—before your wife does.

—Keep Smilin', Dr. R.V. Shrink

Tired of RV pressure

Dear R.V. Shrink:

My husband is constantly worried about our tire pressure. I get so tired of hearing the latest news about tire conditions as we are traveling down the road through some of the most beautiful scenery in the world. It is all my fault. I bought him a tire monitoring system for his birthday. I thought it might prevent him from using his pressure gauge on all of our tires every day. Should I just keep quiet and let him enjoy his tire pressure fixation? It seems the monitor is never perfectly tuned to the tires and he now worries more than before I bought it for him.

—Tired of Pressure in St. Pete

Dear Tired:

I think it was great that you bought your husband a tire monitor.

It can benefit both of you in a safety manner. They are especially useful if you are towing a car behind a motorhome. I have seen motorhomes hauling tow cars with a flat tire and the driver having no clue his vehicle is disintegrating behind him. Tire monitors can be frustrating. Most problems turn out to involve low batteries. The monitor has batteries, the sensors have batteries, and the relays have batteries. They all have to be in good charge for the hardware to communicate with each other. They allow you to set the pressure and temperature threshold for each individual tire, which can often alert you to a pending tire failure. They also have alarm tones to alert you to abrupt changes in same. If you bought your husband a decent system, the monitor should be doing all the work for him. Have him read his manual over carefully and see if he is understanding all the functions the system offers. Monitoring tire pressure and making sure it is always correct will save you money, time and expense in the long run. I would discuss your disgust with the constant tire dialog. Your husband may not realize you are disinterested in his pressure points. Since you bought him this new tool, he may just be making the point that he is using it.

—Keep Smilin', Dr. R.V. Shrink

Sharing our favorite campground with good friends from Canada

RV Christmas Decor

Dear Dr. R.V. Shrink:

It's almost Christmas and I want a tree and lights just like the old days. I thought a wreath on the front of the motorhome would also be fun. The problem is my husband thinks it's crazy. Just because we live in a 29-foot motorhome shouldn't cancel Christmas. I'm not looking for the twin pine that sits at Rockefeller Plaza, I just want a little Christmas tree and a few lights. Is that asking too much?

—Bah Humbug in Hermosa Beach

Dear Bah:

When I was a kid, my dad would buy those pattern kits of wooden choir boys, and nativity scene. He would spend the Fall in his wood shop, cutting and painting. In December he would stake it all out in the front yard and wire it for lights and sound. He had speakers wired directly to his Hammond Organ so he could fill his scene with his favorite Christmas music. I think this might be what you should suggest to your husband. By the time you negotiate your way back to a simple tree, he will probably be more than happy to go out and buy one himself. Today you can buy a fake tree that is already trimmed in lights. They come in all sizes and store easily. You can even find 12 Volt LED lights if you are a boondocker. There is no shortage of Christmas spirit in RV campgrounds. If you don't want to carry a lot of seasonal decor, just park next to someone who does. Last week I saw a couple with a 5th wheel lit up like a casino. They even had a blowup Santa on the roof climbing in a chimney. Don't forget to hang a stocking for your husband with a lump of coal in it.

—Keep Smilin', Dr. R.V. Shrink

Looking for RV nuggets

Dear Dr. R.V. Shrink:

I follow your column each week and find it informative and thought-provoking. However, I cannot always figure out the things you suggest. In the past few weeks my interest was piqued with the suggestion of a Medigap Plan F High Deductible plan, and last week the mining claim idea. I had never heard of either. In researching both I find little information. Do they really exist or do you just make this stuff up?

—Mrs. Doubtfire in Deadwood

Dear Doubt:

Both these ideas are way too bizarre for even me to make up. Let's begin with the fact that signing up for Medicare is not for sissies. I stated in that column that insurance companies function profitably by keeping customers and potential customers confused. There is little money in Plan F HD. Many companies do not really sell it, they just use it as bait to get you to bite. Once they have you on the hook (get you to call) they send you to a high-pressure salesperson, stuffed into a cubical, to sell you something you do not want or need. To make things even more complicated, rates and coverage vary by state and even counties. My suggestion would be to call your state Medicare office and ask them to give you a list of companies that actually say they sell Plan F High Deductible. Your troubles do not stop there. It will be the last thing they try to sell you and the premium will change faster than their lips move. It must be good if they don't want to sell it to you, so stay at it, be persistent. Hang in there like a bulldog. After you get all insured, head for the gold fields so you can pay for your new medical coverage. I am no expert on mining claims. I have met a couple people who have done this and they seem to be happy campers. One bought his claim on eBay. If you check eBay you will see sellers with mining claims up for bid. This looks like the expensive way to stake a claim. Doing your own paperwork and finding your own claim would be much cheaper ($200+). Check with a BLM office near you. From my understanding, you need to work the claim, which might mean using a metal detector occasionally. I have also read that it does not give you the right to a private chunk of land. You only own the mining surface rights. Anyone can come out and camp next to you, they just can't look for your Mother Lode without your permission. Really, that's not so bad. You might get lonely out there looking for nuggets and want a bit of company. Remember, if you find gold, don't tell anyone. If you don't find gold and want to sell your claim, get a gold tooth and smile broadly at each prospective buyer. This may be a way of finding a cheap place to camp in the desert for the winter, but I think staying on BLM land would be a lot easier, with no paperwork. Remember, the guy that made the most money during the Gold Rush was named Levi, and he sold pants.

—Keep Smilin', Dr. R.V. Shrink

Room with a view—Following the Gulf around Florida

Looking for RV Oz

Dear Dr. R.V. Shrink:

We have been 3/4-time RVing for several years. We feel like we have seen everything that interests us. We like biking, hiking, kayaking and nature watching. Our travels have been mostly National Park/Forest hopping. We are at a point in our lives when we would just like to sit somewhere warm and natural for a few months in the winter. We are turned off by commercial RV parks. The South is full of them. We are not into potluck dinners, line dancing, pickle ball and all the rest. We just want dark, quiet nights, natural surroundings, and interaction with like-minded people. Is there such a place, or are we pipe-dreaming? Maybe finding this place with a quaint nearby town is not being realistic. Any advice on how to be happy with what we can find?

—Looking for Oz in Arizona

Dear Ozzie:

I don't think that is asking too much. The problem is finding the right fit. I assume you have considered continuing your present mode of travel and just staying at your favorite parks for the full allowable time limit which is usually 14 days. That would only move you a dozen times a winter from one awesome place to another. You could also consider volunteer work in a park you really love. That would give you the opportunity to stay much longer in one spot. You might consider looking for a home or lot to rent in an area that fits your needs and allows RV parking. If you spend the time and money to become as self-contained as possible you could find a quiet place on BLM land that would allow you to stay much longer. Many sites are near small towns that you might find interesting. I know people that have registered mining claims, just to have privacy and boondock-type surroundings, with room enough to invite friends to stay. You might consider buying or leasing land with others who are looking for the same camping opportunities you are. Having a small private campground with people you enjoy can be a great opportunity to enjoy the place you love, make a small investment, plan your own parking space, and enjoy the things that interest you. Not very different from a condo, a time-share or investing in a lot in an RV park. It just gives you a bit more control over your surroundings. While you contemplate what will make you happy, I would just keep doing longer stays in parks you enjoy. After 14 days, you probably need to dump and water-up anyway. Find the primo parks you love, reserve your whole winter in the sites you like the most, and continue to enjoy the lifestyle you always have.

—Keep Smilin', Dr. R.V. Shrink

RV magical mystery tour

Dear Dr. R.V. Shrink:

We will begin our great RV adventure in about a year. We are what you would call "wet behind the ears" when it comes to RV traveling. My husband thinks it is going to be this magical mystery tour. I think he might be building himself up for disappointment. I am trying to throttle him a bit. Is this unfair? Should I just let him dream his dreams and let him find out the hard way that it's not all utopia out there?

—Balloon Bursting in Baltimore

Dear Bursting:

Don't rain on his parade. It can be whatever he wants it to be. Everyone will create a different experience, pursue different interests, follow different highways, pick different places to camp and live. You two will have to find your own way. I like to think of this lifestyle as utopia. If I were to suggest reading material it wouldn't be a road atlas. I would suggest starting with Steinbeck's "Travels with Charlie." I read it in high school and found it very helpful. I lived in my truck for a summer traveling across America. I used Steinbeck's method of washing my clothes. He hung a plastic bucket with a lid from bungee cords. After a hundred miles of sloshing around you stop and put the rinse water in. It works great. My second suggestion would be one of my favorite writers, William Least Heat-Moon. He will inspire you to look for that which is not obvious as you travel. Start with "Blue Highways," then "Here, There, Elsewhere." If he inspires you then continue with "River-Horse" and "PrairyErth." There is adventure around every bend in the road if you have the right mindset. Don't be afraid to explore, meet people, try new things, expand your horizons. We just set crab traps and caught monster fish off the coast of California, and we don't even like seafood! But now we have stories to tell and memories to tuck away. There may be some trying times. We just drove up a one-lane curvy road to a beautiful National Forest campground. There were a few hairy moments when our motorhome met cars coming down. Sure they think we are nuts, but we are having cocktails tonight in one of the most beautiful places in California. My point is, don't let anxiety turn you into a main road traveler. The magical mystery tour will be found along the "Blue Highways."

—Keep Smilin', Dr. R.V. Shrink

Camping in the sagebrush in the shadow of the Sierra Nevada mountains

Down in the RV dumps

Dear Dr. R.V. Shrink:

We enjoyed your column last week on investing in gas. We don't go that far, but we do like the instant gratification of not having to pay for services that are often free. We use every travel App available to find inexpensive camping, dump stations, gas, and propane. It pays a huge dividend every year. We recently went to a Loves Truck Stop in California that our App said, "Free dump with a fill-up." After filling up we found that the dump costs $5, with or without a fill-up. I feel it was a bait and switch tactic. Do you agree they should honor the promise you find on their website? Maybe I am being petty? Just down the expressway, we found a free state dump station at the next rest area.

—Down five bucks in the dumps

Dear Down:

I think I see your mistake. Correct me if I am wrong, but I have only made a mistake once in my life. I thought I was wrong once, but I was mistaken. Having used both Loves dump stations and many dump Apps, I know that the Apps are not always correct. You should always check with management before assuming the App is correct. Businesses change management and policies all the time. Apps may not always be up to date. They are great if used as a reference, but not gospel. It seems I have had free dumps at Loves in the past, but not recently. They do offer a very convenient island that has a dump, water, and propane all in the same location. A convenient pit stop can be well worth five bucks. They often have good fuel pricing, so a single stop can be very efficient. You can't expect them to honor old or out of date information, but often they will with the least bit of complaint. My suggestion would be to check with the attendant before proceeding. Armed with up-to-date information, you should be able to make the best decision. Next time you are down in the dumps, be sure to use sanitizer.

—Keep Smilin', Dr. R.V. Shrink

RV gasaholic

Dear Dr. R.V. Shrink:

My husband thinks he is Warren Buffet, but in reality, he has a hard time deciding what to take at an "all you can eat" buffet. Since we retired and started living most of the year on the road, he has way too much time on his hands. He is always coming up with cockamamie ideas. Lately, it is saving money on gas. Now that gas is low, he wants to invest in a gasoline option. He says that will lock him in at today's price, so it won't matter how high the price of gas goes, we will be pegged at this low point of entry. Should I just gas him and lock him in at this point. I am at wit's end. I am so sick of hearing this mumbo jumbo. He has no clue exactly how this works. He has never invested in the commodities market. Should I make him go see an adviser? Help me quick.

—Fumed in Fremont

Dear Fumed:

There is a good amount of money made every day in the commodities market. It all comes from the people that make bad judgments. Your husband has no business being in a risky trade he knows nothing about. It's very risky for the pros. If he insists on trying to lock in a profit from the low oil prices of this minute, maybe he should consider something less volatile, like a blue chip oil major. Their stocks are down at this point. They often follow the price of oil. There is nothing to guarantee it won't go lower or be much higher by the time this publishes in a few days. Unlike a futures contract, you and your husband can hang on to a well-managed, dividend-paying stock. When the price of oil goes back up, they will benefit, the stock will most likely appreciate, you will receive a dividend and if you like, you can subtract any profit from your gas bill. If your stock goes south, at least you won't be sitting by a pier somewhere, waiting to take delivery of 42,000 gallons of unleaded fuel your husband bought and refuses to sell at a loss. Don't send him to an adviser. Wall Street is littered with the burnt-out shells of people with advisers. Consider the fact that an adviser or managed fund charging 1.25% annually will cost you $125,000 over 10 years on a $500,000 portfolio @ 8% growth. You can buy a lot of expensive gas with that dough — and your adviser is! Yes, I guess you should just lock him up.

   —Keep Smilin', Dr. R.V. Shrink

Full moon rising over Cottonwood Campground in Big Bend National Park, Texas

Smoke and mirrors

Dear Dr. R.V. Shrink:

I liked your take on Medicare last week, but that is not what makes us nuts. How about taking a shot at cell service. We just started traveling and can't decide what we should do. We have talked to dozens of other RVer's and it seems everyone has their own favorite. There are more cell plan offers than Medicare ever thought of, and we are more confused than our foreign speaking GPS. (That's another story. I won't go there right now). Please give us some advice, or we might just stop communicating with the world.

—Smoke and Mirrors in Minot

Dear Smoke and Mirrors:

Cell plans are much like insurance. Companies have the same business plan, Confuse and Conquer. It takes as much homework to find a deal that fits your needs and budget, as finding a decent policy. To keep your sanity you need to do a few things regularly. The most important would be to read and understand your bill. AT$T (that's not a typo) was just ordered to return to customers north of 100 million dollars for false charges. That money was only returned to people who don't read their bill. Because the people that do, never let them have it in the first place. Verizon has stopped overcharging me because I would call them every month to get the forty cents or a buck back that they overcharged me. No questions asked they would just reimburse my account. Do the math-they have 20+ million customers. If they can slip a few million accounting mistakes past them every month it's really good for the bottom line. Once I discovered how many people don't read their bill, I bought Verizon stock. The dividend keeps rising—I wonder why? The point is-read your bill each month. As for service, you would be better off sticking with the company that has the most coverage. At this time, that would be Verizon. Maybe because they have the most people that don't read their bill. Now if you are feeling a little confused, wait until you go to a Carrier and talk to their sales tag team. Usually, there is a greeter who queues you up to see a sales associate. Then they start convincing you how wonderful their deals are and sell you a device that does everything but wash the dishes for you. It all comes at a steep price. Don't you wonder why they give you free talk and text now? That used to cost big money. Now it's all about data. That's where they nail you. Sometimes you just have to take a leap of faith. You are doing things right so far. Keep talking to people, reading consumer articles and tech news. Things are changing fast. In my humble opinion, I think the best deal going at the time is the Walmart Straight Talk plan. You can buy a smartphone with a Verizon chip, have no contract, and unlimited talk, text, and DATA, for $45 a month, plus tax. It's 3G service and no roaming. No roaming means your phone won't pick up another carrier's tower if you are out of range of your carrier's tower. We are going on our 3rd month of this service with a Verizon phone and have logged over 4,000 miles from the Midwest to the West Coast. We have only been out of service in some of the most remote areas we backpack in. We have never been throttled on our data, and never have to worry about going over. So good luck, read your bill and don't talk on your phone when driving.

—Keep Smilin', Dr. R.V. Shrink

Planned Seniorhood

Dear Dr. R.V. Shrink:

We retired early and took our Social Security at 62. We have been on the road full-time for four years. This year we both have to decide how to take Medicare. It is driving my husband crazy. He says it is more complicated than a corn maze. He has been online studying and stewing about it for two months now and still hasn't come to a decision. Time is running out to make that decision and I can't seem to get him to pull the trigger on one plan or another. Should I lock him in the trailer and refuse to let him out until he decides, or is that too harsh? He doesn't appreciate my input because I haven't studied it at all and have no idea how to proceed. I look to him to make this decision and I don't know how to get him to jump.

—Medinuts in Medford

Dear Medinuts:

The way insurance works is simple. Most companies have a very uncomplicated business plan—Confuse and Conquer. Medicare works the same way. Instead of having basic coverage that just kicks in when you reach 65, they have multiple choice plans, with multiple choice plans within the plans. I can see how your husband is totally confused. The problem is, he has to make his choices.

Everyone has a different set of circumstances, so it takes a bit of homework to figure out which combination of options works best for you. It sounds like he has done his due diligence. Here is how I decided. This may not be your solution, but it may give you some guidance as to how to attack the problem. I found a copy of the Medicare guidebook and read it a couple times. Then I called a local Medicare facility and asked questions on things I found totally confusing. Once things started to focus more, it was not all that confusing for me. I am highly suspect of insurance companies. So when my mailbox started filling up with bazillions of offers to buy into a Medicare Advantage Plan I personally became suspicious. When I called about Medigap Plans I was always being routed to the Advantage cubical of salespeople. This was another red flag for me. As a full-timer, I decided I did not want a network plan. With Original Medicare I can go anywhere I want that accepts it. I also found that with an Advantage Plan I would have to go see doctors A and B before I could see doctor C. If I want to go to doctor C, I would rather go direct. If you want to go with an Advantage Plan, pick one and get it over with, but read the fine print. If you don't want to go with an Advantage Plan, and you stick with Original Medicare, here is a starting point for your husband. You get Medicare A, and Medicare B will come out of your Social Security. Easy so far, right? Now you hit Medicare Plan C. It has a whole alphabet full of sub-plans. You will notice that Plan F is the most expensive because it covers 100% of deductibles and co-pays. What many people miss is that Plan F has a high deductible option (HD). It is a very reasonable premium and tops your cost out at just over $2,100. Out of all the alphabet soup deals I studied, this looked like the best deal for the least dollars. Then we get to Plan D, which stands for DRUGS. By this time you need drugs just to focus and make a decision. If you are in need of regular drugs, you are going to deal with the donut hole for several more years. It won't matter if you are in an Advantage Plan or Original. Most communities have a Senior Help Center that will sit down with you and give you step-by-step walk-through plan options. Another thought for Veterans is the VA can be part or all of your plan if you so choose. I wouldn't lock your husband in the trailer unless you are in there with him. This decision will affect you as much as him. You should be studying this labyrinth of lunacy as hard as he is. Together you can help each other make the best decision that will cover your personal situations.

— Keep Smilin', Dr. R.V. Shrink

Awareness

Shut out of government campgrounds

Dear Dr. R.V. Shrink:

I should probably be writing to my Congressman instead of you, but I've decided to write to both. My wife and I have waited for years to be able to travel during the fall when campgrounds in popular areas are less crowded. Now I am discovering that the government camping sites like National Forest and National Park campgrounds are closing in mid-September to early October. Often we can't get into a park campground because they have only left one loop open. It might as well be the 4th of July, everyone is fighting for a site in a single loop. The weather in areas I am referring to is often mild until late October. I can see the need to cut back on the activities offered during prime time but how hard is it to leave a gate open. I don't care if they shut the water off, close the bathroom, board up the visitor center, and send the seasonal rangers home. Just leave the campground open so I can find a place to park near the places I love to hike. Am I missing something, asking too much, being unreasonable?

—Fall Guy in Freeport

Dear Fall Guy:

It is probably not a bad idea to write your Congressman. What-ever side of the fence your representative resides on, I am almost sure a vote to increase the Park Service budget is not on the top of the priority list. In their defense, I have to say I have noticed the park service monitoring usage and reopening loops, especially on weekends, into the late fall. There is definitely a shift in shoulder season crowds. As more and more seniors retire, shoulder season usage will continue to rise. Many families take advantage of fall weekends to get out and enjoy these same areas. I believe the Park and Forest Service see these same subtle changes and are trying to deal with them and still maintain a balanced budget. I can think of a lot of things the government could cut to pay for better-maintained parks, but don't get me started. Everyone has their own pet projects and needs. I am just grateful so much public land has been set aside in this spectacular country of ours. You may get a clearer picture of what is happening in the park or parks you are referring to by talking to management there. I would start with an explanation from them before I wrote someone in Washington with six aides pumping out form letters. Other than that, use prime season tactics like showing up early or making reservations where you can.

—Keep Smilin', Dr. R.V. Shrink

RV camp scout

Dear Dr. R.V. Shrink:

I know this sounds like small potatoes, but it is just something that bugs me to death. My wife likes to explore campgrounds we stay in before she finally picks a site. Our typical mode of operation is to drop the toad, she goes in to pick a site, then calls or comes back to get me. The problem is, sometimes she's gone a month. Okay, I'm exaggerating. But it does seem like she is gone a long time. I would rather just drive in and look around, pick a site and be done with it. She needs the door facing a certain direction, the motorhome facing a certain direction, the right sun/shade combination, the right distance from lighting, bathroom and noisy trash containers. Should I be thankful or annoyed? At this time I am mostly annoyed.

—Waiting for patience in Pocatello

Dear Pocat:

Sometimes finding utopia takes a few minutes. Part of your problem is you are not keeping your mind busy. While she is gone, do something else. Don't sit in the driver's seat impatiently waiting for her to come back. It will only turn minutes into hours. Many people would give their left lug nut to have an onboard camping planner. It also allows her to see if there are any obstacles that might cause your mothership to have any difficulties maneuvering. I can see her point about the trash containers. Especially the bear-proof containers that sound like a car crash every time someone drops the lid. One thing you may suggest is keeping a log of her favorite sites. In the future, you may return and in many cases, you can reserve the sites you found the most suitable in the past. Many online reservation systems will show a photo of the site, give you a sun/shade rating, length suggestion and more. These can be helpful before you arrive, even as a walk-in, without a reservation. So relax, go with the flow, clean your windshield while she is gone. It's just a perception of time you need to manage. In the end, you probably get the best site available in every campground where you stay.

—Keep Smilin', Dr. R.V. Shrink

When you go Out West—Everyone gets a cowboy hat

RV snow job

Dear Dr. R.V. Shrink:

We travel a lot during the shoulder season in many parts of the country. We find mostly great weather, fewer crowds, and fewer camping hassles. We do encounter the freak snowstorm on occasion. This can usually be anticipated and prepared for. However, my wife insists on having the slides out every night. She does not like dealing with the smaller kitchen area, or climbing over the bed when they are in. When they are out during a snowfall, I have to deal with frozen, snow-covered slides before we can move on. This often means climbing on the roof of the motorhome to broom off whatever ice and snow has accumulated. Wouldn't you say she was being unreasonable?

—Frosty in Snowmass

Dear Frosty:

It seems to me it would be much easier to deal with the kitchen space limitations than the ice and snow build-up on the slides. Most rigs are designed to be very functional with the slides in. I find it wise to pull them in during many weather events. A strong windstorm can drive you crazy with the slide awnings flapping. If you know the chance of snow is almost certain, it only makes sense to pull them in and eliminate the hassle of dealing with the aftermath. Traveling in snow country during the fall season can be very rewarding with spectacular scenery, fewer crowds, and often cheaper rates. It is wise to carry a step ladder. A ladder is convenient for maintenance and reaching tall windows for cleaning. It also comes in handy when you need to deal with your slides. There is also a safety issue here which your wife may pay attention too. If you had to move for some type of emergency and your slides were iced up, it would at the least slow your progress or perhaps end up causing damage to the slides. It is something we all deal with. I personally make sure my slides are clean and there is nothing to impede them every time I extend or retract. Depending on the consistency and quantity of snow, a slide is designed to shed it like water. Knowing the cost of slide repair, I prefer to err on the side of caution and clean the snow off before retracting the slide. The slide awning will be collapsed on the top of the slide and often not retract properly until you remove heavy snow. These issues often come down to common sense. I have left my slides out on many occasions knowing I was going to wait out a snowstorm, warmer weather was forecast or deciding I would deal with the job of cleaning it off. It comes down to a personal choice, but if you are not comfortable dealing with these conditions, pulling them in is as easy as pushing a button. You might want to explain to your wife the danger of climbing around on a slippery RV roof during or after a snowstorm.

—Keep Smilin', Dr. R.V. Shrink

.

Half Lit RV

Dear Dr. R.V. Shrink:

Visiting Seattle, Washington, we found the RV camping options wanting. We finally picked the one closest to our daughter's home and ferry terminal. Like the rest, this one was basically a parking lot with as many RVs jammed into it as possible. To make it resemble a parking lot it even came with dozens of floodlights that lit up the whole area. My husband ended up duct taping black garbage bags over the bedroom windows and vents just to keep the light out during the night. Our rig looked like it had been in an accident. Not only did we pay dearly to stay in this poor excuse for an RV park, but the manager complained about our garbage bag-covered windows and said we would have to remove them. We have just started RVing. Is this what we can expect living this lifestyle?

—Half Lit in Ferryland

Dear Half Lit:

Urban RVing, you will find, is often cramped and costly. It's all about the cost of real estate. You will learn new tricks the more you travel. Let me give you one for the next time you sleep under a floodlight. If your eyelids don't do the job, go to Walmart and buy an eye mask. It's kind of fun. You will think you are sleeping with the Lone Ranger. It will save on garbage bags and duct tape. Camping near a big city will often involve noise pollution, light pollution, air pollution and every other kind of pollution you can think of. It's simple math: multiply numbers-divide resources. If you do not have to be close to the family, hospital, or some event, consider staying farther out of town and commuting in. You will find it much quieter the more rural you get. If you haven't already discovered online resources, start by reading campground reviews. They will give you a much more accurate description of what to expect than the creative marketing presentation of a campground website. A website can make an asphalt parking lot campground sound like Shangri-La. If you spend some time and effort, you can often find a fellow RVer online who lives in the area and will be more than happy to share some insight on where to stay and where to avoid. Try some of the RV forums to present your questions. Don't get discouraged. You will find your favorite little safe harbors to drop anchor. You just need to get more experience under your belt and more miles under your land yacht.

—Keep Smilin', Dr. R.V. Shrink

I met my first Mermaid in 1958—Three generations traveled
from Michigan to Florida

RV crap shoot

Dear Dr. R.V. Shrink:

Before we retired, my wife was a bean counter for one of the
largest accounting firms in the U.S. When it comes to numbers
she is a bit fanatic. Now that we are traveling most of the year in
our motorhome, she categorizes all of our expenditures and keeps
constant track of how much we spend. That is all well and good,
but one of these categories drives me nuts. She is always trying
to keep camping expense in a profit position. The way she plans

on doing this involves casino camping a few times each month. I know as an accountant she should understand odds more than most people, but she loves playing roulette. It is hard for me to argue with her on this point because at this time we are ahead. Applying her roulette winnings to the camping expense column we have an average camping cost of fewer than two dollars a night so far this year. My point is that it can go the other way at any time. She insists she has a system that will cap our losses. How can I convince her that in the end, the house always wins?

—Chipping away at expenses in Laughlin

Dear Laugh:

Let's break this down a bit. The house does not always win. There are numerous casinos that offer overnight parking, many with free hookups. Most are quieter than Walmart, have security, and welcome travelers. It's a win-win situation as long as you don't go inside. Another way to look at it is entertainment. If you go inside and set your gambling limit at your camping savings, you break even. You don't explain your wife's plan on capping her losses; I assume it is similar to my point of breaking even. Casinos are popping up everywhere. There are several websites that offer updated information on those that extend the welcome mat to those looking for overnight parking. They each have a different set of rules. Some expect you to come in and sign up for a Player's Club Card, but most just direct you to an RV parking area. In your wife's defense, roulette seems to be the best odds of any gaming. If she just plays black and red she would have just less than a 50-50 chance. I don't think the odds get any better than that; it's all downhill from there. I agree with you in the fact that eventually the house always wins, because most people don't know when to fold 'em, know when to walk away, or know when to run. However,

I get the impression your wife has her own little system. It sounds like she enjoys playing, enjoys calculating her wins and losses against her camping expenses, and seems to think she will cap her losses if camping gets to be more expensive spinning the wheel than not. I have termed trying to find a campground opening in the reservation system, "Campground Bingo." This puts a new spin on that term. I wouldn't worry too much about your wife's gambling habit unless she insists on casino camping every night, or gets addicted to wheeling and dealing so much she forgets about her cap system. There is one other downside. When she comes back to the RV she will smell like smoke and it isn't from a campfire.

—Keep Smilin', Dr. R.V. Shrink

RV cheap tricks

Dear Dr. R.V. Shrink:

My husband thinks he's a bonafide RV mechanic. He will work on a problem until he's spent more money than having a qualified RV mechanic do the job. He refuses to have anyone work on our rig until he has exhausted his possible do-it-yourself fixes. He has a one-track mind, so whenever he is on a mission to fix something I've lost him completely until it gets solved. He is always online looking for advice, tricks of the trade, and cheap fixes. Wouldn't it be wiser to just have a mechanic repair our rig? Wouldn't it be cheaper in the long run, less hassle and headache?

—Cheap Tricks in Tampa

Dear Tricks:

Some people want to be a rock star and others an RV mechanic. I think your husband is on the right track. Even if it ends up costing him more money to completely solve a problem, he has educated himself for future situations. Online advice is priceless. There is hardly a subject not covered. We all experience the same mechanical problems sooner or later. You will find people online describing your precise issue, how to fix it, and what parts you will need. I find it amazing. Your husband's laser focus can be looked at in another way. During the time you lose his attention, you could be stuck in a motel, waiting for a service technician to call and tell you they finally figured out your problem. Some of these people have to think about it for as long as your husband and try as many parts and solutions. The only difference is, they have the meter running at about $100 bucks an hour. Many RV problems come down to plug and play electronic boards in current models. You can often find great trouble-shooting help from aftermarket board companies like Dinosaur. Your husband is building experience that will pay off handsomely in the future. You should be happy and encourage him. A lot of women who used to go for handsome are now looking for handy. You had better keep a close eye on him.

—Keep Smilin', Dr. R.V. Shrink

Airstream International Rally—Hershey, PA in 1961
Chocolate factory and amusement park—every kid's dream

Private vs Public

Dear Dr. R.V. Shrink:

We have been traveling for almost nine months. We bought a fifth-wheel, a new truck, and all the toys. We plan to travel for several years and look for some special place to spend winters, once we have seen all the sights. The problem is campground choice. I like to stay in commercial campgrounds with all the amenities and my husband likes to rough it in remote scenic campgrounds. He told me, "If I wanted to spend my retirement sardined into a shoebox campsite I would have bought a mobile home." He complains that we are so close to neighbors he can hear them talking, smell them smoking, and listen to their TV programs. I don't think it's that bad. I get bored sitting out in the woods, desert, and ocean by ourselves. Are we normal? Does everyone have this problem?

—Unhappy Campers in Coos Bay

Dear Unhappy:

As with most disagreements, it takes compromise. If only everyone had your small problem to deal with. I'm sure you have favorite campgrounds you both have enjoyed. Start with those. Look for commercial parks with bigger lots. Often you have to pay a premium for more open space, but perhaps it's worth it to buffer yourselves from the talk, smoke, and TV. As for being bored in remote public campgrounds, work on that problem. It's surprising how many people dive into this RV lifestyle without giving any thought as to what comes next. Is travel your only hobby? If you are bored you may need to explore interests that you can take on the road. Join activities and meet fellow travelers. Play cards, explore bike trails, swim, dance and go out for dinner and a movie. Living on the road should not be much different than the life you lived before shoving off. It just encompasses new places, new friends, new experiences. Your choice of campsites is a personal matter involving cost, locations, hookups, and so much more. There is no shortage of places to camp, park or even put down semi-permanent roots. I think if you work together to choose camping options, your husband will find parks he can live with, and you will find rural settings that keep your interest.

—Keep Smilin', Dr. R.V. Shrink

RV road race

Dear Dr. R.V. Shrink:

We just bought a travel trailer. My husband and I have always wanted to travel around the United States. I was always thinking to do this it would only take a couple months. I had no idea he was thinking a whole year. I can't imagine being away from home for an entire year. Do you think he is exaggerating? It has been a constant argument since we discovered our individual concepts of the time it would take to see the country in our new abode on the road. Please help us sort this out.

—Sixty Day Tripper in Delaware

Dear Sixty:

I think you are both way off the mark. So far it has taken me sixty years. Everyone has a different slant on the definition of "seeing the country." Two months will possibly just whet your appetite. It will be a snapshot, not a full-length movie. If you want to jump on the super slab and see the whole country at 70 m.p.h. you can probably do the miles in a couple months. If you want to travel the Blue Highways, stop and smell the roses, it may take years. My suggestion would be to pick a section of the country you would both like to explore and not try to paint on such a broad canvas. Exploring the country is like eating an elephant, "one bite at a time." Even sectioning off a piece of the geography will not solve your time dilemma. You will have to decide what you want to explore—the big cities, parks, natural areas, museums, historical sites, eateries, rural communities, or a combination of these and more. If you have the luxury of not setting a time limit, just begin at the beginning and let the trip unfold before you. My wife and I decided to travel for a year when we were 25—we didn't come back for a decade. The journey will be what you make it. Setting limits and boundaries can hamper the experience of letting the trip take you, instead of you taking the trip.

—Keep Smilin', Dr. R.V. Shrink

The RV chores are quick and easy once you refine your technique

Feeling the RV heat

Dear Dr. R.V. Shrink:

We have a forced air furnace in our motorhome. It works fine. My husband thinks we need to add a catalytic heater. He claims the forced air furnace fan drains our batteries too fast. I don't want another gas appliance in our small space, it doesn't look that safe, and I doubt it will make much difference in battery drain. He is insisting we need it. I need some help in convincing him this is not a rational idea. Please help me.

—Feeling the Heat in Helena

Dear Helena:

It is a rational idea. Your husband is right about the battery drain. The catalytic heater would be cheaper to operate, give constant heat, and create zero battery drain. Cons: it would produce more condensation, necessitate some added ventilation, and add a substantial investment to buy and plumb into your motorhome. You have gas equipment in your rig now, but perhaps you are not comfortable with this addition. If that is the case, you can add solar instead. A small solar investment will replace the battery drain from the furnace fan. When comparing prices between the two, don't forget to add the cost of plumbing the gas into the motorhome. You will spend as much on brass fittings and copper lines as you will on the heater itself. I wish I would have bought brass fittings instead of stock for my retirement. I would be rich beyond my wildest dreams. Brass is the new gold. If installed properly and used properly, one of the auxiliary heaters is a fine addition to any RV. We personally use all three, solar, catalytic and forced air and enjoy the freedom of not worrying about keeping a healthy battery charge. Your husband is on the right track. I have often seen people leaving campgrounds early because of dead batteries. They have to drive or use a generator to power a battery charger. This often happens when there is a cold spell and the furnace is working overtime. A small investment in solar will pay for itself over time. Calculate how often you find yourself paying for an electric site so you can charge your battery bank. If you like to dry camp a lot, your payoff will occur much quicker. Heaters like Big Buddy and Wave are radiant heat. They transfer heat to surrounding objects, which in turn release heat into the space you occupy. It is a very comfortable heat but does entail finding a space that will be safe, convenient and aesthetically pleasing. Good luck. Discuss this with your husband and maybe you will warm up to the idea of an added heat source.

—Keep Smilin', Dr. R.V. Shrink

RV labor force

Dear Dr. R.V. Shrink:

My wife and I are entering the intersection of agreement and disagreement. We are both moving at full speed ahead and I fear a catastrophic collision is imminent. She wants to agree to a host position in Arizona this winter that works out to a full-time position at a volunteers wage. I agree we need to reduce our living expenses, but to work full-time for half the cost of full hookups works out to about a dollar an hour. I think the owners are taking advantage of the supply of retired RV owners willing to work for rent. My wife says she gets bored and needs to work. The problem is the job offer is for a couple. That involves me working the same amount of hours. My wife refuses to comprehend that we are actually bartering 320 hours of work for a $300 savings in rent. How do I explain to her my unwillingness to work for slave wages without the conversation turning into a shouting match?

—Labor Dispute in Douglas

Dear Doug:

I think you are wise to look for a compromise before you both reach the intersection at the same moment. It is pretty simple math. It is also supply and demand, an economic model of price determination in the market. You can't blame the park owner for making the best business decision for himself. If he can find people willing to work those hours for that compensation, he is going to take advantage of that. One of the elements that has evolved from the thousands of boomers retiring and traveling has been "volunteerism." That has evolved into "work camping." Both the public and private sector have embraced the idea of part-time workers who live full or part-time in an RV. The number of people looking for these types of positions continues to grow as more and more people take to the RV lifestyle. The two of you will have to work out a compromise. That usually involves both parties getting some of what it demands. Have you discussed looking for a park that offers better bartering terms? Have you considered one or both of you looking for a better paying position nearby this park? You could then stay busy, pay full price for your rent, and come out ahead financially. A great part of the RV lifestyle is portability. Take your skills and desires and transfer them to another geographic location that may offer better compensation and still give you the climate you are seeking for the winter. Along with the fact that supply is beginning to erode away demand in this labor market, new opportunities are being created constantly. Corporate America is beginning to appreciate the possibilities of utilizing seniors enjoying the RV lifestyle in filling gaps in the workforce. Amazon is the perfect example with a seasonal need for holiday workers. The Oil and Gas industry has found a great fit using RV owners to monitor production site gates. You can find great natural camping, bartering with state and federal parks and wildlife refuges for various part-time hours, in trade for full-hookups. Like any other position in the workforce, sometimes it takes time and patience to end up with what you ultimately desire. Try a few jobs, build a network of friends, gather information, discover the little nuances of how the system works and focus on the positions you want. It is often easier for a couple to find a work camper job than a single applicant, but there are thousands of singles doing exactly the same thing. If you can afford to be choosy, take your time, start early, apply for multiple positions and take the one that appeals to both of you. Closing your eyes to the conflict, with your feet in the carburetor, moving headlong into the intersection, will only result in casualties. Don't be crash dummies. Practice "safe service" when scouting for a work camping billet.

— Keep Smilin', Dr. R.V. Shrink

Lakefront property site with no taxes—That's the RV Lifestyle
Alma, Nebraska Corps of Engineers park

RV Cat-astrophe

Dear Dr. R.V. Shrink:

We have been traveling in a 29 ft. travel trailer for a couple years. We said when we first retired this would be our first step into RVing. It was not expensive. We wanted to see what others were doing, get some opinions, and try the lifestyle without making a huge investment. We are now convinced that this is the lifestyle for us. We have also decided that we would prefer a motorhome about the same length as our trailer. We started looking for a lightly used motorhome. Recently we found one that was a steal. It was a divorce situation. The wife ended up with it in the divorce and never wanted the thing, to begin with. She is a very motivated seller. It was everything we wanted in a floor plan, price, options, and color. The problem is, my husband is allergic to cats. This unit had been occupied by the owners two cats on quite a few occasions. He claims symptoms every time he walks into the unit. We have looked at it three times and each time he has complained. I told him we could have it professionally cleaned, but he says he is not willing to gamble on the fact that cleaning would completely eliminate the problem. It is such a great buy and I think we should take the chance. This has caused a lot of heated debate between us. Am I being unreasonable? Should I drop my campaign to buy this unit and try to make it work for us?

—Cats in the Cradle in Coeur d'Alene

Dear Cats:

Everyone with allergies will have different levels of severity. It sounds like your husband may be at the top of the scale. It would be a gamble to buy the unit and discover it did not solve the problem. There are several ways to approach the issue. If the seller would work with you and hold the sale, you could spend the money to have it professionally cleaned. That way you would know ahead of time. It would be a win-win situation. The owner would have a professionally cleaned unit whether you purchased it or not. You could buy it outright and work on it yourself. If it is truly a great buy, you could always resell it, perhaps at a profit. It is hard to say what all would need to be done. You may have to replace bedding, furniture, and floor coverings, even after cleaning. I have witnessed people walking into professionally cleaned RVs and immediately asking, "Has this unit had cats living in it?" Unless you are sensitive to the presence of some pets, you would not understand completely. If you can't work something out that eliminates the reaction your husband is experiencing, this unit is not the great deal you think in your circumstances. Move on and forget it. It will be a great deal for someone without your husband's condition.

 —Keep Smilin', Dr. R.V. Shrink

RV camping confrontation

Dear Dr. R.V. Shrink:

 We have retired and live in a small travel trailer. It is just the right size for us. We have been on the road for almost a year and we are loving it. The only problem I have is my wife. She gets annoyed by our camping neighbors way too often. I am a retired State Police Officer, but she thinks I'm still on the job. I admit we do get some real winners parking next to us at times. We were just in Glacier National Park and our neighbor was breaking just about all the rules at one time. It was more than my wife could handle, so I went over and had a talk with him. That did not go well. We were in a no generator zone, no firewood gathering, and a no burn ban was on. This nut case had his generator fired up to run his electric chainsaw. He was cutting down trees so he could feed his enormous campfire. After I talked to him and he told me to buzz off, the campground host showed up. He did listen to the host and stopped his insanity. If I was the sheriff in town, he would have been fined so heavily he would have needed a loan to get home. I don't want my wife unhappy. I don't want to be the law east or west of the Pecos, and I do not want to be annoyed. Am I asking too much for the campground administrators to do their job? Isn't it part of what I pay for in my fees? Things are so lax that people keep pushing the limits of noise, rule-breaking, and litter. No consequences just embolden them. Do you think it's my background? Do I need some professional help in letting my past training go?

—Cop off the beaten path

Dear Cop:

It is not just your background. We all deal with this insanity on a regular basis. We watched something similar one night in a Forest Service campground. The host came by, hesitated a moment, and moved along. I heard him say, mostly to himself, "People, ya gotta hate 'em." In fairness to the host, it is not his job to police the area either. But it is his job to call in backup. Now with so many camping areas going to a concession status, jurisdiction keeps getting cloudier and law enforcement less available. If you are going to do anything, I would suggest you report to the nearest local management. At that point, you have done what you can.

Hang up the badge. If you can't seem to hang up the badge, become a host. Just because it is not the host's job to confront unruly people, it doesn't mean it can't be. Every campground should have a chain of command. Someone's in charge. Things can be done, it's just not your job as a registered camper. You will not be considered someone of authority, just a complaining neighbor. You will find things get resolved much quicker by going through the proper channels. It is much better for your wife to be a bit frustrated than you in a verbal or physical confrontation with someone who obviously isn't too squared away, to begin with.

—Keep Smilin', Dr. R.V. Shrink

Awakening

RV Little Big Mansion

Dear Dr. R.V. Shrink:

My wife is dragging her feet when it comes to buying an RV. We have been planning this move into retirement for a number of years. We plan to keep our home, but live in the RV for most months of the year. Her problem seems to be space. She doesn't want a big RV, but she wants lots of storage, cooking area, bath, and bedroom. That is an impossible combination. Please give me some reasoning firepower so we can get past this perception obstacle in our road to retirement.

—Little Big Mansion on Wheels

Dear Little Big Man:

If you have never had an RV it will take some adjustments. I do not know how your wife defines "Big." Just about every manufacturer has added slideouts to their models. This makes a huge difference in what is being hauled and what is stretched out at the destination. This could help in meeting her standards for size and space. The other things to consider when shopping for a rig would be storage. Being organized in a small space is key to successful living. Having plenty of storage will be a significant help in staying organized. You will find the smaller the unit, the less space is dedicated to storage. Something with basement storage (storage space under the floor) will make a huge difference in what you end up stepping over. (Pun intended) You need to look at as many floor plans as possible, with your list of needs, likes, and dislikes. I can't guarantee you are going to find a unit that will make your wife happy. She needs to be open-minded about the fact that this is not going to be a 1500 square foot house on wheels. Most people in the retirement stage of life begin to downsize, throw out ballast they have collected over the years, and start sharing family heirlooms with children and family members. My grandfather in his last years told me to tell him what I wanted of his and he would put my name on it. I told him I wanted the safe. I should have been more specific. I did get the safe, but it was empty. Another point that may help your cause is housekeeping. You will both find it much easier to clean and maintain an RV than a home. Once you actually get on the road you will find you have much more time on your hands to explore and do things you truly enjoy. You can always start small and work your way up. Once your wife is comfortable with traveling in a smaller rig, she may find it more realistic to bump up a bit. Looking at units will give you an idea of how just three feet can gain you more elbow room in various living spaces. In most situations, you will also spend more time outdoors than you normally would at home.

—Keep Smilin', Dr. R.V. Shrink

RV Shiner

Dear Dr. R.V. Shrink:

Your recent letter, about constantly cleaning the RV, struck a chord with me. I am not a neat freak or constant cleaner, but I do like a nice looking rig. I think my problem is, I can't make a decision. I read way too many RV forums. Lately, it has been cleaning related. My wife makes me come home once a year to mow the lawn. When it gets knee high, people start to wonder. She met a local woman who asked her where she lived. When my wife told her, the woman was so relieved. She told my wife she thought two old people died in our house and no one had found them yet. To get to my point, I use this pit stop to do yearly maintenance on our rig. Most campgrounds do not allow RV washing. I want to refinish the exterior, but I am perplexed as to what route to take. The previous owner used Poliglow finish on it and made it look like a million bucks. It was wearing in places so I just stripped the whole rig. It has been a real bear getting that stuff off. I used all the solution from the Poly people, then tried ammonia, and ended up using ZEP floor stripper. It was the only thing I found that would really cut the Poliglow. It would be easy to just re-apply Poliglow, but I hate the thought of having to strip it again in a few years. After reading a week's worth of RV forum suggestions, I just can't think straight anymore. It's like I am being pulled in several different directions at once. I have never been like this. I am usually focused and can make good decisions without second thoughts. Is this a problem many RV owners have, or a rare condition that is only haunting me?

—Poli Perplexed in PA

Dear Poli:

You are not alone. Many RV models are unpainted gel coat with decals. Most manufacturers do not recommend wax on decals. Trying to wax around them is like painting by number. Some opt to use products like ProtectAll and Aerospace 303. These have a short UV protection life, as they weather off quickly. Poliglow and other remedies like floor polishes do make a rig shine like a new penny, offer some UV protection and can last a long time if applied properly and maintained adequately. I began my working career as an Airstream Shine Boy. As a kid, I used Met-All with a carpet affixed to a floor sander to de-oxidize aluminum trailers. I then used flour to absorb it and buff it out. Airstream eventually went to an acrylic clear coat. With my first motorhome, I waxed everything twice a year. The decals went south and nothing would bring them back. In my opinion, most decals are only going to look good for about 5 years no matter what you do, short of polishing once a month with products like 303 or spending big bucks for a full paint job. That would cut way into my backpacking time and budget. You are not alone in your dilemma. Personally, I'm a Poliglow owner. I have had the misfortune of having to strip a few I have bought used. It is no fun. Like all finishes, it wears away eventually. It needs a couple maintenance coats per year. The secret is to do the prep work correctly. It's not for everyone. But after trying it all, I find it the least time-consuming. I didn't buy an RV to be a slave to it. It sounds like you already schedule a time to do yearly maintenance, this might be the way to go. The other methods are equally effective and you actually build up muscle stamina with the constant motions involved in waxing and polishing. You can start looking buff just from buffing. If you talk to enough people I bet you will find others with methods you will find as interesting as all those that have you confused from the other RV forums. If one of these does not convince you, I would suggest you write them all on scraps of paper, put them in a scrub bucket, hold the bucket over your head, reach up and pick one out.

—Keep Smilin', Dr. R.V. Shrink

Crabbing in Bodega Bay in California—Life is Good

OCD RV MD

Dear Dr. R.V. Shrink:

My husband is obsessive-compulsive when it comes to groom-ing. I'm not talking about his hair. It's our motorhome. If it is not shining like a new penny, he is out there scrubbing on it, polishing it, and spraying everything from the roof to rubber seals with some magic juice he carries with us. Is this normal behavior? Do all RV owners spend so much time tinkering? He says it is just "pride in ownership." Let's hear your two cents worth.

— OCD in B.C.

150

Dear OCD:

RV and boat owners are in the same club. It's called the "Scrub Club." To be a member in good standing you have to spend a good portion of your time maintaining your investment. As long as it does not interfere with other activities you enjoy together, I think it is very normal behavior. You should be happy that you have a partner that enjoys maintaining your rolling abode. Just the habit of going over the rig to clean makes him aware of many other things that might need attention. It also familiarizes him with your unit. If he were at home he would be doing home maintenance. This is your home on wheels and it is exposed to many deteriorating elements as you travel around the country. Just keeping bug juice off the front of a rig can be a full-time job. Leaving dried carcasses there will eventually deteriorate the finish. I am going to assume the magic juice he uses is a product like Aerospace 303 or Armor All. It has to be done often, but it is like putting SP 40 sunblock on your rig. It protects gel coat, plastics, rubber seals and more. It also keeps the suicidal insects from sticking too badly. It is unwise to wax over decals, so his magic juice protects them and gives everything else a nice shine. The downside is, it needs to be applied often. A busy mind is a happy mind, so unless it is interfering with your schedule, stop fretting about it. Embrace his enthusiasm, it is slowing the depreciation on your investment and keeping your husband happy and healthy doing what he seems to enjoy.

—Keep Smilin', Dr. R.V. Shrink

Spilling the beans

Dear Dr. R.V. Shrink:

My wife says I am a constant "I told you so" person. I try not to be, but I feel I am entitled to my opinion. The latest is cooking in our motorhome while we are driving down the road. My wife wanted to make baked beans so they would be done when we reached our destination. I said it didn't sound like a good idea. She insisted. Before the beans had a chance to begin setting up, we hit a long 7% grade. As you can imagine the beans spilled over in the oven, began to burn, and created a horrible baked on mess. That, of course, is when the "I told you so" came rushing out of me. She thinks it was a fluke and insists she will try it again on better roads. Can you explain to her that this is not about being right or wrong, it's about safety?

—Burnt Beans in Big Bear

Dear Burnt Beans:

I can tell you the National Propane Association would not recommend it. There are many things that can go wrong and burnt beans are the least of them. I will tell you that many people I have known do cook while traveling, but then again some people I know start campfires with gasoline. Our mothers always told us not to play with matches, but most of us ended up with burns on our fingers anyway. Why not try a different approach with your wife. Next time you are at a Flying J, buy a 12volt crock pot. It will sit safely in the sink and slow cook a great meal all day long. Much safer and much cheaper than using propane. When I graduated from high school in '68, that summer I lived in a 1964 Suburban and enjoyed backpacking through the West. Back then they would pump your gas and check your oil. I stopped one day and the attendant asked if I would like my oil checked. I said, "Yes, and will you also check the meatloaf and see if it's done." He opened the hood and exclaimed, "He does have meatloaf under here!" Probably not the best idea cooking greasy food on a V-6 block, but I was young and foolish. Get a crock pot and play it safe. If you do not take my advice, don't say I didn't tell you so.

—Keep Smilin', Dr. R.V. Shrink

This truck was used to guard the Berlin Wall—Now it is an RV traveling the world

RV utopia

Dear Dr. R.V. Shrink:

We are in the advanced stage of our RV lifestyle. We are not yet ready to give up our gypsy life, but we are ready to find a more permanent mooring. We have been all over North America during the last decade. Now we would like to find a few perfect spots to spend the seasons and park for longer periods of time. The problem is we can't agree on those geographical locations. My wife likes the Southwest, I like the wild parts of Florida. She likes summers in the Midwest, I like the mountains. She likes the fall colors of Vermont, I like Colorado. We are always arguing about where to throw out the anchor. I think we should invest in property in a couple of agreed upon areas, but so far we have not found the perfect paradise for both of us. Can you offer any advice on settling this settlement issue?

—Looking for utopia with little hopia

Dear Looking:

I will try to help with what little information you have provided. Maybe you don't have as complicated an issue as you think. Perhaps you are not totally committed to settling as you think. If your health is good and you still enjoy travel, maybe you should visit the places on both lists, just stay longer than in the past. Take turns on the seasonal stops. Often you will discover a change in attitude about a place, once you have spent more time, made friends, discovered new interests and understand seasonal weather patterns. You will have a totally different attitude about a location when you have spent a couple months instead of a couple weeks. You may find it harder to settle down for longer periods of time if you have been moving constantly for a decade. Take it slow, grow into this new lifestyle. It will not be all that different. You still live on wheels and can make change by simply unhooking the utilities and hooking the RV. I would not advise investing in property until you have both invested a fair amount of time in an area and agree that this is where you could possibly spread some roots. It is important that you both stay active, so make sure the areas you decide on offer something for both of you to thrive. You will most likely discover there is no such place as utopia, but with a little planning and some trial and error, you might come close. Good luck.

—Keep Smilin', Dr. R.V. Shrink

RV gas app

Dear Dr. R.V. Shrink:

You are always suggesting people use gas apps to find the best prices. I find these programs very inaccurate. One of the more popular would be Gas Buddy. I'm parked at a Walmart for the night. Right across the street is a Shell Station. Gas Buddy is telling me that the price of gas there is $3.69 per gallon. The Shell sign says it's $3.87. Which one do you think I'm going to be asked to pay? Perhaps all this online, high tech, wizardry isn't all it's cracked up to be. Am I doing something wrong, or is the 18 cent difference the fudge factor? My mother always said I asked too many questions. Maybe I'm incurable.

—Skeptic in Schenectady

Dear Skeptic:

You have to take everything with a grain of salt. It's good to maintain a degree of skepticism. My point is that information gathering will help you make better decisions, so keep asking questions and looking for answers. It's very healthy. Using a tool such as this app might not be as precise as we would like it, but on average it will save you money. The way I use these gas apps is to let it help target the lowest priced gas stations in a geographical area. No matter what the price, that station will often still have the lowest price. The gas price heat map of the entire U.S. will help you identify the cheapest route, illustrate the areas with the highest gas tax, and help you plan your best pit stops. Most of these apps work off data from credit card swipes and usually keeps them quite current. You should love Google. It's full of answers. I use Google for my doctor, mechanic, vet, tour guide—the list goes on. I just visited my motorhome manufacturer and they were too busy to have a tech talk to me about my room slides, but Google's YouTube had a guy standing by who was glad to walk me through the slide adjustment procedure. I also use the many RV forums when I have a mechanical problem I can't figure out. I read them all because some people will complain if they are "hung with a new rope." Like the gas app, I take a consensus of opinion before I proceed.

—Keep Smilin', Dr. R.V. Shrink

Exploring Capital Reef National Park, Utah
A warm spring day camped in a lush oasis in 1979

RV plumbing problem

Dear Dr. R.V. Shrink:

When my husband talked me into buying an RV and traveling he said the bathroom facilities would be just as comfortable and convenient as our home. It all looked good, but now we often have to put up with a plugged up toilet. I didn't sign up for this. He keeps telling me he has it figured out. Everything moves along fine for a while, but then our holding tank seems to get bound up again. Is there an Ex-Lax for RV's? I am enjoying the lifestyle but this little glitch is turning me off. My husband says I am making a mountain out of a molehill. Am I being unreasonable? I just want to get rid of the mountainous molehill in the black water tank. Is that asking too much?

—Stink hole in Yellowstone

Dear Stink:

Raising a little stink will often bring an issue to a head. If this is the only problem you have with the RV lifestyle, you have had a smooth move. The transition often causes problems that couples cannot find any common ground. In your case, I have lots of ideas that should solve your problem. There is a science to getting along with your RV plumbing. Several things to be aware of include using toilet paper that breaks down easily. A simple test is to put a few sheets in a jar and shake it. It should fall apart quickly. Another problem is using too little water, trying to extend the black water capacity. Use plenty of water when flushing and always put a couple of bowls full in the tank after dumping. Pouring hot water directly down the bowl opening will help unclog present blockage, but care in how you use the system will assure fewer problems in the future. Some black water tanks are plumbed for rinsing, many companies offer chemicals and tank enzymes, but using the proper method of caring for the waste system will solve the majority of your problems and give you some relief, no pun intended.

—Keep Smilin', Dr. R.V. Shrink

RV park amenities

Dear Dr. R.V. Shrink:

I get real irritated when I feel like I've been scammed. Lately, it's happened when I spend time at commercial RV campgrounds. I use online website information to make my decision where to stay. Often they list all their amenities with enough creative writing to make the intent vague. Often "Wi-Fi Available" means just that. It's available for an extra daily charge, or you need to sign up with a local service. We just paid for a month in Florida with the expressed understanding that the pool, hot tub, recreation hall, and wood shop would be available to us through the month of April. Mid-month they started mothballing these facilities for the season. It took a lot of complaining to convince them we had a verbal agreement plus advertising stating that we could expect these amenities to be available to us for the entire month. I'm starting to feel like an old curmudgeon, but if I don't complain they take advantage. My wife says I should just "go with the flow." But I always seem to blow. What say you?

—Laid Back Screamin' in the Sunshine State

Dear Screamin':

It takes some time to see a pattern, but once you find it, make a simple call and ask the hard questions. Wi-Fi is very important in this day and age. Data is expensive, so park owners may opt to charge extra as they do electricity. Regardless, it should be clearly stated in their list of amenities. You need to perform due diligence when investigating charges before making your parking decisions. As far as getting cranky, it can sometimes become necessary. We just spent a month in a park with absentee management. The volunteers running the place were mathematically challenged. I first had to give them a lesson in prorating a monthly charge, and then in placing the decimal point in kilowatts on the electrical bill. Their math added $40 dollars to my monthly bill and $30 dollars to my electric bill. I was flabbergasted that they were running a park with hundreds of spaces and did not understand how to do sixth-grade math. It could be good for the bottom line of the business if customers do not pay attention to their charges. I know they thought I was a jerk, but they probably didn't like their math teacher in school either. Once you have an understanding of what the actual charges and amenities are you have every right to expect just that. I would suggest you start your questioning with a very understanding attitude. If all else fails sometimes a lively debate will begin to get results.

—Keep Smilin', Dr. R.V. Shrink

Taking the RV on a boat ride can transport you to some very exotic places

Happiness is California in the rearview mirror

Dear Dr. R.V. Shrink:

My husband will not spend much time in California. I have family there and I love visiting the Redwoods. We arrived for a visit this spring and our first fill up was $4.99 a gallon. Our first campground was $35.00 a night with electric service so low our surge protector would not allow it to fire up the motorhome. As we left the campground we went to dump and it was $10 extra to dump. My husband refused to pay the additional fee. Later that day we found another dump for $12. He was ready to head for the state line, but I made him settle down. Can you explain to him that California is no different than any other state?

—California Dreamin' in Lee Vining

Dear Lee:

I'm sure if you continued on, you would have found cheaper gas on the other side of the Sierras. I can't say that California is like all other states. It's all about supply and demand. Since there are 20 million+ people living in just the southern half of California, everything is more expensive from taxes to dump stations. Wait until you stop at a California state park —don't forget Redwoods National Park campgrounds are all state campgrounds. My only advice would be to plan ahead as much as possible. Buy gas before crossing the border, use your RV dump apps to find cheap or free dumpsites. Some California rest stops have free dumps. Use apps that help locate the cheapest gas, campgrounds, and propane. The cost will continue to rise, so your best offense is a good defense. California is not like Vegas. What happens in California does not stay in California. Just remember, in ten years these will look like bargain basement prices. The good ole days are now. Enjoy them while you can.

—Keep Smilin', Dr. R.V. Shrink

Smokin' down the road

Dear Dr. R.V. Shrink:

I'm a recovered "inhaleaholic." I smoked for thirty years. Now that my wife and I have retired I would like her to quit also. We just bought a new fifth wheel and take delivery by midsummer. I think it would be great if she would quit before we start using the new rig but she is not open to the idea. She says it is too late to quit, too difficult, and too frustrating to think about. I totally understand I was there once. Should I give up or keep trying to convince her?

—Butting Heads in Tobacco Row

Dear Butting:

I can think of several good reasons to quit smoking besides your wife's health. Start with the resale of the rig. When I was a kid I worked for the biggest Airstream dealer in the country. In the sixties, the interior was a fleck paint coating. When we took in used units it was my job to refurbish, shine the exterior and clean the interior. A trailer owned by a smoker would be the biggest challenge to clean. I would spray the painted surface with a cleaner and the yellow nicotine would melt off. It was so thick you could see a distinct line where I had cleaned. Today most RV's have more fabric interiors that will hold the nicotine smell forever. If she cannot quit, you may want to work out an agreement where she smokes outside only or perhaps tries the new vapor E-cigarettes.

Unlike Bill Clinton, I "really" never have inhaled, but I can imagine how hard it is to quit any type of nicotine delivery system. In the long run, you will save a lot of money giving up this expensive habit that may eventually increase your medical expenses also. If safety, health and cleaning reasons will not help your wife decide to quit, and she doesn't go for the smoking outside program, you will have a second-hand fifth wheel full of second-hand smoke. Good luck.

    —Keep Smilin', Dr. R.V. Shrink

Rocky Mountain High—Taking a breather after a long hard climb

RV Bookie Joint

Dear Dr. R.V. Shrink:

My wife thinks we are a rolling library. Our travel trailer reminds me of the "I Love Lucy" episode where she sneaks rocks into the trailer without Ricky knowing. I am an avid reader also, but I jettison books I have already finished. I donate them to libraries or thrift stores or give them to friends. My wife thinks she might want to read them all again and stuffs them in every nook and cranny she can find. I think she is a literary packrat. She thinks this behavior is perfectly normal. Can you help me knock some common sense into her?

—Bookie Joint on Wheels in West Texas

Dear Bookie:

First of all, "we don't knock." I would think in this day and age you can both have your way. Have you ever suggested she buy a Kindle or other such device for her reading pleasure? A lot of people say they do not like reading on a screen device, but don't knock it until you've tried it. You can put hundreds of books on such a device, or add cloud service or memory and keep unlimited numbers. That will solve the storage problem. You can get free or reasonably priced ebooks from Amazon, BookBub, and even borrow from your library. Amazon also has the Kindle Owners' Lending Library with over 500,000 free Kindle books available. This is a lending process so you will only be able to borrow the book, not keep it. You'll need to be an Amazon Prime member to take advantage of it. I'm sure there are other sources I've never used. You can even share books with friends. You will also find many RV maintenance and campground directories downloadable online and search active. Most RVers find being paperless with banking, taxes, manuals, and all other reading materials save time, helps organize and becomes a great convenience. In your case, it is also going to save so much gas when you remove the Smithsonian Institute from your trailer. Buy her a unit as a gift and get her hooked on Nook. It may take a little time, but my guess is she will wean her way off the hard copies pretty darn quick. She doesn't have to go "cold turkey." There are still a lot of good book deals at thrift stores. I just bought a great book in New Mexico at a thrift shop. It is the story of Butch Cassidy after his misspent youth. Supposedly he wasn't killed in Bolivia. Anyway, it was a buck. They were having a special and knocked 40% off. Then they looked at me and gave me the automatic, you don't even have to ask, 50% Senior Discount. They even had a deeper handicapped discount and I'm blind in one eye. I didn't go there. I was happy with my thirty cent book. The secret is to get your wife to stop hoarding. If you can get her to take one load of books to Goodwill and she comes home with two loads, she may need more therapy than I am capable of administering.

—Keep Smilin' Dr. R.V. Shrink

No way to run an RV railroad

Dear Dr. R.V. Shrink:

My husband just had another episode of management frustration. He retired as a business consultant and cannot seem to let go now that we are traveling full-time. We tried to book a couple weeks in the campground at the Grand Canyon. The reservation.gov site would only let us book 7 consecutive days on the only site we could find available. He called reservation.gov to find out if it was that particular site, or were all sites restricted to 7 days. They did not know. That started it. He thought they should know or be able to find out. They offered no other assistance and told him to call the park. A call to the park only made it worse. Like many corporations, the National Park system doesn't want to talk to people either. They hook you up to several minutes of voicemail choices and then you reach a dead end with no option to talk to a real person. That only makes him more determined. He Googled for an hour and finally found a news release about a new Assistant Superintendent at the park. He called the media specialist and found she was stationed at the Superintendent's office in the park. She tried to get rid of him, but he insisted she find an answer for him or connect him to the Superintendent. Finally, he found out that all sites at the Grand Canyon are limited to 7 days because it is such a popular destination. This is just one example of how he won't let poor communications, poor marketing, poor organization, and poor information services slip by without making a fuss. How can I get him to relax and go with the flow?

—Karen at the Canyon

Dear Karen:

Maybe it is not a problem. Perhaps he enjoys the challenge. I like the way he thinks. When I have a problem with a Corp. or a government agency, I always start at the top and work my way down. It's so easy today to find out the name of the CEO. You never get to talk to the CEO but you always get your answer or problem solved so much faster that way. I agree with him that if some person in a New York city cubical is going to run the park service campgrounds they should have all the answers or have access to them. If his focus on things running properly is upsetting you, then you should create a time when he can work on these extracurricular activities without involving you or giving you a blow-by-blow account of what is happening. Some people would love to have an onboard wagon master that could solve all the problems, get all the answers and work out a route through the hostile territories of business and government. An onslaught of government bureaucracy can be very frustrating. Now the park service is handing over so many management activities to concessioners that it creates more opportunity for buck-passing. It can get overwhelming.

 —Keep Smilin', Dr. R.V. Shrink

Apprehension

RV woman

Dear Dr. R.V. Shrink:

I am trying to learn everything about our RV just in case my husband keels over one day and I have to get this monster (RV) home. I seldom drive, never dump the holding tanks and never fill with water. Those are the things I have been practicing. The problem is there are always men standing around telling me what I am doing wrong before I even get a chance to figure things out on my own. If I hear "righty tighty, lefty loosey" one more time, I'm going to give someone a "dirty swirly." Am I being too thin-skinned? I just want some space to make my own mistakes and learn from experience.

—RV woman in Willcox

Dear RV woman:

Good for you. I think everyone on board should know everything about the ship. If the Captain falls overboard, the First Mate can still get the ship back to port. I'm thinking most people that give advice, whether asked for or not, mean well. You will have to make your own judgment calls on where your advice is coming from and how it's delivered. But I agree with the learning from experience. These are mostly simple chores but repetitive practice makes perfect. Various dump stations, water facilities, and road conditions call for different approaches to the same procedures. It is important to experience them all. Working as a husband/wife team is very important - especially when backing into a site. Remember, the helpful person that might come over to help back you in has nothing invested. If someone was trying to tell me how to dump my rig, I would just step aside and ask them to show me. The "dirty swirly" sounds like a bad idea. I'm sure you could be charged with some kind of brown collar crime.

—Keep Smilin', Dr. R.V. Shrink

RV tax

Dear Dr. R.V. Shrink:

We are about to spend ten times more on a new motorhome than our first house cost forty years ago. It makes me a little uneasy to spend this kind of money on a vehicle that will be traveling down the road depreciating. It has always been my husband's dream. It sounds appealing to me so I am throwing caution to the wind and sailing away with him. However, he is trying to penny pinch on taxes using what I would call borderline legal schemes and dishonest practices. He has been looking into setting up a Montana LLC. We live in Ohio. He says it would cost us about twelve hundred dollars and save us thousands. Then he talked to a friend that never renews his license plates. The theory is: pay the fine instead of the tax. I have been very supportive of this new lifestyle but my husband is upset because I won't go along with the tax cheating. Am I being too closed minded? Are others doing this? Is it legal?

— Honest Abby in Akron

Dear Abby:

Yes, others are doing this. Many are very nervous now because various states have caught on to the practice and are now pursuing these folks for back taxes and penalties. As for the plate renewal, I would think that would catch up to you very quickly in this age of computer data. I would assume law enforcement could run your plate for various reasons on the fly in any state and know immediately that you are running on expired plates. If you are heading out on a grand adventure, spending big bucks for a new home on wheels, and looking forward to a relaxing lifestyle, do you really want to be looking over your shoulder all the time wondering if someone is after you? You have to pay to play. My suggestion would be to follow the rules and travel worry-free. If, however, you sell your property in Ohio and change your residency to a state with little or no sales tax, you can enjoy those savings without fear of prosecution. Many people who are full-timers use services available in states like South Dakota to establish residency, mail forwarding service, and taxes. Taxes are a necessary evil. I was an accountant in the Marine Corps, so if you want to know where your taxes go, just ask me. If you want to use Military accounting practices to save money, just start at the bottom line with what you want back and work up.

—Keep Smilin', Dr. R.V. Shrink

Traveling when our daughters crib was an Airstream bathtub

RV sound waves

Dear Dr. R.V. Shrink:

I know people have complained about this in the past, but it irks me to no end when I have to listen to another camper's music. There should be a "No Tolerance" rule. I just spent two days feeling my rig vibrate from a deep bass, rap-crap song, over and over. The host said it was perfectly legal during the hours they were listening. Sound is so invasive. If people want to listen to whatever music turns them on, let them stay home in the privacy of their home. Why should I be exposed to it? Am I just an old curmudgeon getting ornery in my old age? In some campgrounds, I wish I had already gone deaf. In this case, it wouldn't have helped - I could feel it!

—Bad Vibrating in Valencia

Dear Bad Vibes:

I don't think this is an age issue, but it is an age-old complaint. You will run into all kinds of people and campground management variations while on the road. I would have to say, the majority have some pretty decent control over what goes on in a campground setting. That being said, when you reach a destination you are looking forward to and find yourself in the vicinity of a boom box, it can be frustrating. I agree that sounds are invasive and need to be controlled. Most campgrounds have set hours for generators and loud noise of any kind. That, however, does not solve the problem of those seeking some quiet and solitude during daylight hours. Focusing on music I would agree with more volume control. I have witnessed people trying to out blast each other. You are not going to change management attitude often. I always vote with my feet (wheels). I have even asked for a refund in the past to leave early. To some, camping with Bob Seger belting "Horizontal Bop" is relaxing. If they are within the rules and regulations of the campground, don't look for the host to give you much satisfaction, relocate and chalk it off as bad timing. You might say you are just skipping the beat.

—Keep Smilin', Dr. R.V. Shrink

Locked Out Dear

Dr. R.V. Shrink:

I am so mad I could spit. My husband said I should write to you and vent. I think I should write to you so that I can warn other campers of this possible circumstance. We were visiting Patagonia Lake State Park in Arizona. Like many State Parks around the country, Patagonia has a gate that closes at night. When you register, most parks give you a gate code for entering after hours. At Patagonia Lake, the gate was a long way back from the entrance station and the campground loops. It was a sliding gate and very inconspicuous. We never gave it much thought. We had been to other Arizona State Parks with no gates. We met friends from home for dinner in town one night. When we returned to the campground at 11 pm the gate was closed. There was no one around to let us in. We were never told about a curfew. It was in the information we received when we entered the park, but we never read it. I just think it is important enough that park employees should give people a verbal warning that the park gate closes at 10 pm and there is no way in after that time, except to park your vehicle outside the gate and walk all the way into the camping area in the dark. When we finally made it home I needed a stiff drink just to get to sleep. A gate code would be a much better idea, in my opinion. When I made the suggestion in the morning, I was told the park brochure explained all the park rules.

—Locked and Loaded in Lodi

Dear Loaded:

The majority of gated parks do have a code, which makes perfect sense. I have no idea why this park would have a gate without a code. It is close to the border of Mexico and maybe there is a reason I am not aware of. No matter the case, I agree a verbal warning of awareness to every campground guest only makes sense. Some people for various health reasons would not be able to walk that distance. One thing you might try in the future would be several code combinations if there is a keypad. I have done this a couple times in Florida State Parks when I have left my code information back at the motorhome. Not wanting to walk a mile in the dark I tried 911, 411 etc... Most gates have an easy access code for local emergency personnel to access the park. Often they end in 11. Sometimes people do slide in behind paying guests when a gate opens. If the park has had problems in the past it may be the reason for the aggressive gate policy they have set. Because it is so unusual, I would think a verbal explanation to each and every camper should be mandatory. I know you'll drink to that.

—Keep Smilin', Dr. R.V. Shrink

The cathouse RV—Florida artist's roving studio
in Cape Coral, Florida

Joining the RV club

Dear Dr. R.V. Shrink:

We are not yet in the club. We want to be full-time RVers but my wife thinks she will be lonely. It's not that she doesn't enjoy my company, she just doesn't want to be stuck with me 24/7 without some variety of friends. I have been trying to convince her that we will meet other fellow travelers and locals wherever we wander. Am I just wishful thinking or do most people find sparking friendship on the road a common occurrence?

— Lonely Hearts in Loveland

Dear Lonely:

Trust me, it is not wishful thinking. If you are outgoing at all you will collect so many new, awesome friends, your dance card will be constantly full. You will often run into the same friends over and over as you are traveling in the same geographical areas. You will find not only camaraderie but a sharing of great information on maintenance, gear, camping opportunities, recreational options, the list goes on. In my humble opinion, the very best aspect of this RV lifestyle is the wonderful people you meet along the way, from all over the world. Let me just give you one recent example. I just started hiking the Arizona Trail from the Mexico border fence in Coronado National Monument to Utah. The problem was having my wife drop me off on the border and then worrying about whether she made it back to our motorhome safely. We were parked in a National Forest campground 20 miles north of the border. I thought about trying to hitchhike down. The dirt road south is heavily used, but it's all border patrol trucks. There were only a few other campers, but we decided to walk around the campground and see if anyone might be going down to the

Monument and if I might catch a ride. The first group we ran into were not only the nicest and friendliest people, but they were also Arizona Trail members. They were section hiking the first section of the trail. They had a shuttle service from Tucson picking them up in the morning and driving them to the border trailhead and said I was more than welcome to join them. We had so much in common, and laughed and told life stories. I call this "Trail Magic" when things happen unexpectedly while long-distance hiking. You will find this same magic wherever you travel if you are open to it.

—Keep Smilin', Dr. R.V. Shrink

RV movie night

Dear Dr. R.V. Shrink:

We have just started traveling and living in a pickup camper several months a year. We have two slides and find it very comfortable. At home we always watch movies. We love movies. On the road, we find we seldom can. We are camping off the grid most of the time. My husband does not want to pay for satellite TV. We never stay in commercial parks with cable. Seldom do we find a town with a movie theater unless we wander into a big city. I miss my movies. My husband says it is not so important. I don't think we have to give up something we both enjoy just because we want to see the rural and natural areas of the country. Am I asking too much? Don't you think we could find a solution? My husband is the tech guy, but he just doesn't seem interested in working on a solution to this problem.

—Oscar the Grouch

Dear Oscar:

This is not a difficult tech fix. When the sun drops early in the winter sky it is often enjoyable to go to the movies in your RV, no matter where it is parked. I will give you a few ideas to pass on to your tech guy and maybe he will become interested in tackling the project. Not knowing what you now have on board, I will throw out a few hardware/software additions you may or may not already have. You can watch movies from a computer very easily or, for about thirty bucks, cable it to a newer flat screen TV. If you don't have a DVD/VCR player, pick one up at a second-hand store. Every thrift store has a mountain of VCR movies that no one wants anymore. They are usually about fifty cents apiece. That's pretty cheap entertainment. Libraries often have tons of movies. Some will let you check them out as a visitor, but if not there is another solution. Some will comment that this is illegal and the FBI will track you down and send you to an RV park with walls topped with concertina wire. But, it is only truly illegal if you are profiting from breaking the copyright law. My suggestion is only allowing you to decide when you want to watch a movie you legally have access to. What you will need is a small hard drive. You can find one at Best Buy for about thirty bucks. It will have a Terabyte of storage, enough for a thousand movies. Rent movies or borrow them from libraries. Download a free software app called HandBrake. This will allow you to transfer movies to your computer or the new hard drive. Your entertainment center, or one you add, will not draw much 12v power. If you have strong batteries and a small inverter you will be able to watch hours of movies without firing up a generator or having electric service. If you find you are running low on 12v power, add a panel or two of solar. The solar will be the best investment you can make for the type of camping you are doing. Popcorn is something you will have to work out on your own. Various methods for making the best popcorn will have to be another column.

—Keep Smilin', Dr. R.V. Shrink

Business meeting with Chuck Woodbury of RVtravel.com
The office is where you find an empty picnic table

Waste Management

Dear Dr. R.V. Shrink:

My wife finds it embarrassing that I haul our waste across the campground in a plastic container with wheels. She thinks we should break camp, hitch up the trailer and haul the whole rig over to the dump. We spend most of the winter in one spot without a sewer hook-up. The dump station is only 25 yards away. I don't mind dealing with the chore. Everything is clean and controlled. It doesn't make a mess. I am sure a million people have these containers. I have used all the reasoning I can muster to convince her this is a normal campground activity. I told her I was writing to you for therapy. Could you give some advice on "to haul or haul not?"

—Wasting Away in Margaritaville

Dear Wasting:

I would say you have nothing to hide. You might as well haul it over to the dump in your underwear. Everyone knows what's in that "honey wagon." They sell those things in all sizes. This year I met a guy in Big Bend National Park that built fresh and waste water tanks in his pickup bed. He is a little less conspicuous, but everyone knows what he's hauling. I can't think of anyone that is not producing the stuff. Someone has to be the delivery person. Your wife should just be glad you haven't asked her to take turns making runs. You've got the runs and she's embarrassed - that stinks. If you can't work this out, my only other solution would be a Sewer Solution RV macerator. I have one for certain situations and it works like a charm. It is only about a hundred bucks but needs a water source to operate. When at home I move waste from my tanks a couple hundred feet to my septic. Water breaks down the waste and then moves it along a 3/4 inch hose. If you are only 25 yards from a sewer connection or dump station this would be a perfect solution for you.

—Keep Smilin', Dr. R.V. Shrink

RV weatherman

Dear Dr. R.V. Shrink:

I am married to a weatherman. He is now retired and we travel most of the year in a 31 ft. Airstream. He is still a full-time weatherman, he just doesn't get paid anymore. Instead of reporting the weather to millions, he only reports to me and our surrounding campsite neighbors. His routine is the same every morning. He gets up at dark-thirty. He puts on coffee. He makes toast under the smoke alarm. He checks all his gadgets, barometer, wind antenna, various thermometers, and his rain gauge. Then he studies his favorite national weather sites online. By the time I get out of bed, he has a prediction. I put up with all this craziness because it's his passion and he is happy. However, I think he drives our neighbors nuts. I notice when we are walking around a campground people see us coming and make dodging maneuvers. He thinks it is all in my imagination. How can I convince him that not everyone is interested in his weather predictions any longer?

—Not the Foggiest in Forest City

Dear Foggy:

Most of your neighbors living the RV lifestyle probably use the touchy-feely weather system. If the heater kicks on in the morning, it's cold. If you hear pitter-patter on the roof, it's raining. If the awning is flapping, it's windy. It's great that he has a hobby he enjoys, can do anywhere you go, and you never have to worry about losing your rig to a tornado. So the only problem seems to be neighbor annoyance. Every campground has a resident annoyer and sometimes you can handle them if they are not parked ten feet away and at your site, every time your foot hits the ground. Making your husband aware of the fact that

180

he might be annoying some people with too much information should be the first step in curing his over-exuberance. If he just can't control himself you may need to point out more examples of people avoiding you after the first contact. Meeting people while traveling is one of the greatest benefits of this lifestyle. You will not mesh gears with everyone, but if you are never making any friends, it might be your husband is still partly cloudy on his ability to read people's reactions to his constant reporting. If he won't listen, give him the hot tongue and cold shoulder until he becomes a bit less windy.

   —Keep Smilin', Dr. R.V. Shrink

Homemade teardrop with a slideout and French doors
You can have it your way

RV wedgie

Dear Dr. R.V. Shrink:

My wife and I have spent most of the winter in a fourteen-foot travel trailer with two dogs. We just wanted to see if we would enjoy this RV lifestyle. We do not. I think it is because we started the experiment with a camper that is too small. I could kick myself. It was my idea not to spend a lot of money on a bigger rig until we knew if we were going to like traveling this way or not. Now I think we would love it if we had more room. My wife is just plain fed up with the whole experience. I can't convince her that most of our problems and discomfort have developed because of our cramped quarters. We thought we were going to arrive in the sunny south to paradise and the temperature would be perfect every day. We discovered that it can often be cold and we end up trapped in our little box. I jokingly call it "two dog days" but my wife fails to see the humor in it. Any suggestions on how to proceed in my attempt to convince her it could be a totally enjoyable adventure if we just had a bigger rig?

—Cramped in Las Cruces

Dear Cramped:

First, tell her she is your main squeeze. See if that breaks the ice or your jaw. To proceed from there I would go for a long walk around the campground. If the small space is truly the only problem, you and your wife should be able to look around any campground and observe how others are coping. The choice of RV floor plan's is endless. You should be able to find one that would fit your personal needs. Some people need more space than others. Walking the campground and studying RV options is a hobby for many new RVers. It is a great way to compare what particular things you dislike about your setup and what you may need to solve them. Once you get a 14 ft. trailer started down the road, it won't cost much more to roll a 24 ft. That extra ten feet can give you a bigger kitchen, a bigger bath, bigger sleeping quarters, bigger living space all around depending on the floor plan you choose. You can take a horse to water but you can't make it drink. If your wife finds other issues with this lifestyle other than cramped quarters, a rock star bus won't solve your problems. You need to have a heart to heart talk, discover the real issues and tackle them one at a time. If you can get out of the dog house, you both might find this is the perfect lifestyle.

— Keep Smilin', Dr. R.V. Shrink

It's 5 o'clock somewhere

Dear Dr. R.V. Shrink:

Now that my husband and I are retired and traveling full-time, he never wears a watch anymore. Every time I ask him what time it is, he never knows. He wore a watch for 40 years. Wouldn't you think that would establish a habit? He says he doesn't care what time it is anymore. That sounds cute, but having a watch doesn't necessarily put you on a schedule. Am I being silly? Do all retirees dispose of their timepiece? I thought the old tradition was to receive a gold watch when you retired.

—Timed out in Tucson

Dear Tucson:

This sounds like an easy fix. Buy yourself a watch. I think it's time for a change. If he has been the timekeeper for 40 years, you do the next 40 then switch. I don't know where the tradition of getting a gold watch at retirement started. I know my dad received

183

one from the telephone company. Today retirees are just happy if they get their pension. Actually, a watch is not as common as it used to be. Some kids can't even tell time if it's not digital. Like so many other devices - cameras, GPS, flashlights, radios, and calculators are all being replaced with Smartphones. Retirees now should get Golden Google Glasses or at least a Smartwatch. I think one of you should carry the time. You don't want to miss cocktail hour. Of course, it's always 5 o'clock somewhere!

—Keep Smilin', Dr. R.V. Shrink

My brother had a tendency to drive when no one was looking

RV theft

Dear Dr. R.V. Shrink:

I learned a lot last week reading various comments to your column on securing the "toad." You might also want to mention tow vehicles. We had our pickup stolen right out of a busy campground. Locked up, no key inside, never found. I never gave it a thought before it happened to me. Now I use a kill switch and a wheel lock. My wife thinks I am a bit paranoid about the whole issue. We were made whole by the insurance company, but you never recover the time, effort and mental strain of being targeted by thieves and having to replace a vehicle. The experience can really put a damper on your travel experience.

—Ripped off in Rockford

Dear Rip:

Your experience is not uncommon. We are presently camped in Big Bend National Park. We met a couple last week with a beautiful 5th Wheel and a new Ford Dually all decked out for towing. They had found a great deal on the truck with extremely low miles. We got their email so that we could keep in touch. Unfortunately, the first email we received reported they had their truck stolen a couple days later in a San Antonio city parking area. Ford pickups are at the top of the stolen vehicle list in the US, but any vehicle can be a target. Manufacturers are adding techie devices to make it harder to accomplish, but an accomplished thief is hard to deter. I personally do not put any trust in electronic security devices. I have had tow truck drivers open my vehicle without getting out of their cab. If they have some type of scanning device that opens vehicles you can bet the bad guys have them too. If you read RV forums you will get some varied and great advice from people who have given a lot of thought to holding on to what they have. The National Parks actually have a lot of crime. The bad guys know that people are traveling and often have their guard down. Common sense and staying alert can save a lot of grief.

—Keep Smilin', Dr. R.V. Shrink

Don't worry, be happy

Dear Dr. R.V. Shrink:

We travel in a Class "C" motorhome and pull a small sedan. My husband is always paranoid that someone is going to steal the car. If we stop for the night at a Walmart or other stopover, he pulls the keys. I think we should leave them in the ignition in the correct position so that if we have to leave in the middle of the night we do not have to exit the motorhome. His arguments are that the battery can drain and someone might be tempted to steal the car when they see the keys. I say let them have the car. It would be more dangerous to go out in the middle of the night and fool with it. Am I the one being paranoid? Do most people lock everything down at night? Should we both just "chill" and not worry so much?

—Nervous Nelly and Bullheaded Bill in Biloxi

Dear Nelly:

RV travel should first and foremost be relaxing and enjoyable. There is no guarantee you are not going to be a crime victim whether you are traveling or at home at the mall. I have only met one couple that lost their toad. They stopped to shop at a Walmart in Mexico. That proves it can happen. I find most Walmarts that allow overnight camping very safe. They are well lit, have security cameras, and may even have security guards. You make a good point about not having to exit the motorhome in the middle of the night if asked to leave a site. If someone were up to no good, they could easily decommission your vehicles some other way. If they are after your toad they are probably going to get it one way or another. My personal mode of operation is to leave the toad in the tow positions. That means the key is in the ignition. With a good battery, you should be able to drive a few days without draining the battery, but a simple kill switch is cheap insurance. It not only ensures you will not drain your battery, it is also another deterrence for a thief. You can make your own for about ten bucks or buy one for fifty. I suggest you take all the precautions, then just relax. Make sure your storage doors are locked, your car is locked, don't leave expensive electronic devices out in the open, and be alert to any situation that doesn't feel right. We spend most months every year on the road and have never had an incident. When making time or a pit stop for groceries we have stayed at many non-campground parking areas. We talk to other RVers every day. I seldom hear of any problems. Again, life offers no guarantees, but don't dwell on being a victim. If you find that you are not comfortable in these sites it might be easier on you to always find official camping sites.

—Keep Smilin', Dr. R.V. Shrink

Circumspection

Cold Cats in Texas

Dear Dr. R.V. Shrink:

As this Arctic Vortex reached way down here to South Texas and grabbed hold with its icy hand, we had a hard time getting propane when we needed it the most. Not because of supply and demand like other parts of the country, we just couldn't find a gas attendant that wanted to come out of their warm office and fill a small motorhome tank. They made all kinds of excuses. I stopped four times in one morning between Bay City, Texas and Corpus Christi. The one that put me over the edge was the Ace Hardware in Rockport, Tx. I finally had two people show up to fill me. They looked like they might freeze to death. It was hovering dangerously around 38 degrees. When I stepped out of the motorhome I was asked if I had any pets. Since our cat was waving at them from the dash, I said yes. The woman said I had to have all people and pets out of the vehicle before I could be filled with propane. I've been at this RVing for a lot of years and I have never heard that one before. I wasn't about to bring out two nervous cats and take a chance of them getting away. I told them to keep their gas, which was music to their ears. I hardly got the words out of my mouth before they were back in the warmth of the store. Am I the only one who has ever heard of this rule? Should I be more understanding of the cold weather challenged? I thought it was pretty obvious that they didn't want to stand in the cold and fill me.

—Frosted in Fulton

Dear Frosty:

That is a new one on me. I have been filling for 50 years and have never heard that one before. Let's start with some common sense, propane fill rules that may or may not be regulation. If you fill ten times in ten different places you will have ten different experiences. It is best to have your own safety rules with you. It is not uncommon to have a propane attendant that has no idea how the equipment works. Your first clue is when they don't know where to attach the filler hose. Many don't know the 80 percent rule and have no clue there is a reason for it. Most tanks are manufactured with some type of overfill float but don't assume an attendant cannot overfill your tank. Even if I stop at an actual propane dealer, I still watch the whole procedure and make sure they are doing it properly. At a gas station outside of Glacier National Park, I had a guy overfill my tank years ago. As the sun rose and things started heating up the propane expanded and it sounded like someone was firing a shotgun in the cab. I suggest you shut off all gas appliances, all passengers exit the vehicle, shut off the main valve at the tank, and watch the attendant like a hawk. Now, as for your recent situation. I called the business you mentioned and at first they were sticking to the pet story. When I asked where I could find this regulation, they started backing water. Wait though, there is more to this story than meets the cat's eye. I then called the Texas National Propane Gas Association. I was told that Texas does require pets to be removed before filling.

I asked about house plants, but she wasn't sure. You will probably never have this happen again in a hundred years, but this particular business seems to be on top of things. I will give them credit for following the rules set forth and assume they follow all other procedures. Probably not a bad place to fill up, but hide the cat first. My Irish grandmother always said, "A little white lie is always better than a big fight."

—Keep Smilin', Dr. R.V. Shrink

RV train wreck

Dear Dr. R.V. Shrink:

My wife bought me a new GPS for Christmas. It was an expensive, big rig model. It is supposed to have all the latest information to keep me from driving our 40 ft. motorhome and toad into areas that are too narrow, too low, etc... Now I am more frustrated than ever. Not only are we out the money for this "special" device, but it is no more accurate than the cheap one I used prior. Besides that, it just sent me down a dead end street in New Orleans and I left the top handrail of my ladder on a low tree branch. My wife says I may not be cut out for RV travel, or that we need to downsize. I love this big rig, but I find myself nervous as a cat under a rocking chair when I get this train on the wrong track. Am I just a novice, nervous Nelly? Will it get better once I get a few more miles under my belt? Should I start looking for a smaller rig?

—Train Wreck in Treme'

Dear Train Wreck:

Your concerns are fairly normal. Let's start out with using a GPS. If this can solve your problem it will be a lot cheaper than taking a bath on trading down. A GPS can be a valuable tool if used properly. Nothing is foolproof. My suggestion on using high-tech navigation is to use everything available. Even after updating my GPS I consider it only 70% accurate. Study your proposed route using other programs that are free. Google maps and free GPS apps give varied formats. You can also use Google Earth to fly into congested areas and get a visual idea of what you will run into. Don't fall blindly in love with the voice on your GPS and take its directions as gospel. If that doesn't work out for you, perhaps downsizing will. There is a huge difference in maneuvering a 30 ft. rig vs. a 40 ft. It may be worth your while to take a driving course if you haven't already. Many dealers offer that option to new owners. If you have never driven a vehicle of that size you will discover there is a learning curve. A few driving tips that you could glean from an instructor or fellow campers will make you much more proficient. You will also learn that one size does not fit all (campgrounds). The larger you get, the more restricted you become no matter how sharp your driving skills. Dolly Parton's dad always tried to convince her that you can't put 20 pounds of mud in a 5-pound sack. Same can be said for trying to put a 40 ft. motorhome in a 24 ft. space. Everyone has their own comfort level. Find yours so you can enjoy your travels and not have to deal with a case of nerves every time you get behind the wheel.

—Keep Smilin', Dr. R.V. Shrink

When RVing to Alaska meant 1,200 miles of dirt road

Unbalanced Toad

Dear Dr. R.V. Shrink:

My husband is an idiot savant, minus the savant part. We are towing a small sedan behind our motorhome. The car started acting strangely. It developed a wobble at slow speeds. At first, we thought it was the roads we were driving on, but it turns out to be an issue with the car. My husband hates to deal with businesses on the road he is not familiar with. He studies any problem for hours before he acts. In this case, he finally decided we had a tire issue. He went and had two new tires put on and the tire dealer told him he also had a bent wheel. The dealer didn't sell wheels, so we just

ended up with two new tires we probably didn't need and still have a wobble. Now he is back studying the problem again. I figure by the time he has it figured out we will have invested in two more tires, a wheel and maybe still have a wobble. I think we should figure out what the problem really is, then spend the money to fix it. He thinks we should study the problem some more. How do I convince him we are doing this all bass-ackwards?
—Unbalanced in Biloxi

Dear Unbalanced:
   You make this sound much easier than it is. I think you are lucky to have a husband that likes to study the problem. It is hard to do business on the road. I like to think that most people are basically honest, but often they are studying the problem too, using your money. The problem you describe is not an easy one to determine sometimes. Your wobble could be caused by a mechanical problem such as a bearing, tie-rod, or any number of front-end alignment parts. It could be a tire with belt separation, or out of round. If a tire dealer thinks you have a bent rim, let's hope that is all it is. Most boneyards will sell you a used wheel with a money-back guarantee if the tire service finds it too is bent. If your tires have a lot of miles on them, replacing them is a good start and great insurance that they are not going to cause you more issues if they fail while being towed. I think your husband deserves more credit than you give him. He has studied the problem, he has sought out a professional opinion, he has made the first purchase attempt at fixing the problem, and he has discovered possible additional causes. Often the problem can be multiple issues. I would not wait long to get to the bottom of the problem. Towing a vehicle with issues is just asking for trouble. I would suggest second and third opinions with brake and alignment services and additional tire

professionals. Unless you have an automotive Ouija board, I would suggest you give your husband a bit more respect and credit. He doesn't sound like he is just throwing money at the problem, but going at it in a practical way.

    —Keep Smilin', Dr. R.V. Shrink

R.V. Shrink Qualifications

Dear Dr. R.V. Shrink:

    I want to ask you a question, but I feel I should know if you are a qualified RV shrink before I trust your advice. I have read many of your columns and it seems to contain good common sense. Lately, I have seen comments from readers accusing you of being a quack. That makes me a little nervous. If you could give me a little background information to assure me, I would greatly appreciate it. Thank you in advance.

    —Doubting Thomas, Tacoma, WA

Dear Thomas:

    I graduated from USMC at the top of my class. It is also known as the "School of Hard Knocks." I received a tremendous amount of on-the-job training. It is a very specialized program that is literally drilled into you. I could not have graduated without the skills I would need to go out into the field and help others. As for my RV background, it started late in my life. It wasn't until I was six that my parents and grandparents bought an Airstream travel trailer. When I was seven I found a guy under the back-end of our trailer, lying on his back, studying our septic system. My dad asked him what he was doing. He said, "I think I can make a better dump valve than this." We were in a Michigan State Park. The guy's name was Frank Sargent. He was an engineer with AC Spark

Plug. He later started a small company called Thedford. He was from Thedford County Michigan. (Just a little history lesson.)Also, Wally Byam taught my brother how to open a locked trailer door without a key. A wrecked trailer came into the factory one day and it was locked. Wally gave the knob a rabbit punch from underneath and it opened right up. My brother picked right up on that. In fact, he knocked several knobs off our trailer before my dad broke him of the habit. As a teenager, I worked all through high school for the largest Airstream dealer in the country, Warner Trailer Sales in Pontiac, MI. Many of our customers were GM engineers developing Wide-Track Pontiacs and other gear that would advance the RV industry. I used to polish Max Bowen's Airstream once a year. You might recognize that name if you have an Atwood Bowen water heater. He and his son also developed Fort Wilderness for Disney. (Another history lesson.)One of the most important lessons I learned from hanging around the trailer sales was this: Don't wait until your 65 to retire. I started right away. I bought the 1964 GMC Suburban that we used to haul trailers up from the Jackson Center, Ohio factory. My dad and I made it into a camper. I didn't even wait for my high school graduation ceremony. I lit out for a summer of camping and backpacking all the way to the West coast and home through Canada. That didn't quite cure me. I got married when I was 24 and told my wife we should travel for a year. We bought an Avion and didn't come back for a decade. Since that time we have had an Airstream and now a motorhome. I have seen many changes in the RV industry, both from a camping and equipment viewpoint. I also spent 22 years publishing "The Dick E. Bird News," mostly baloney, with a few facts. Included was a "Dear Dick E. Bird" column. They used to call me a quack then too.
　—Keep Smilin', Dr. R.V. Shrink

Your RV can release your inner Van Gogh
or at least your trailer Gogh

RV campground critiquing

Dear Dr. R.V. Shrink:

My wife and I love the RV lifestyle. We hope to visit every National Park in the country and all the other interesting points along the way. Although we stay in many wonderful state and national park campgrounds, my wife has developed an annoying hobby of critiquing each site we occupy. She can always find fault with a site no matter how perfect I think it might be. Recently, she could hear the hand drier sound from a nearby restroom. She said it sounded like a pressure washer outside the motorhome every time someone dried their hands. She grades them by size, how close the neighbors are, what kind of view they have, shade, sun, road noise, management attitude, cleanliness, price, the list goes on. It drives me nuts. There is no such thing as perfect. I tell her you have to take the good with the bad and ugly. Can you help me with her attitude adjustment?

—Judgement Day in Daytona

Dear Judge:

Before you cure your wife of her little idiosyncrasy, could you send me her list? I know several people that would love to have it. I think your wife is just more open than the rest of us in this department. We are all looking for the perfect site. I know many people who have learned to work the new reservation system to their advantage. They continually update their campground directories with personal information of what they consider the best site locations in each park they visit. This enables them to reserve that site well in advance if they know they are going to travel that way again. Most people keep this information pretty close to the vest. As competition heats up for campsites around the country, knowledge is King. The same goes for finding and recording great little county, city and local parks that are often overlooked when passing through an area. You can find a lot of information online at sites like freecampgrounds.com, but you have to do more homework to really find the gems. It's called experience. As long as your wife isn't carping about every site you park in, I would encourage her critiquing. If you wanted to share that info online or around the campfire, you will find many people interested and eager to hear your input.

—Keep Smilin', Dr. R.V. Shrink

Peace, Love and RV Tranquility

Dear Dr. R.V. Shrink:

I'm in my late 50's and met a wonderful old hippie who has great social security. We have so much in common and have decided we'd like to be traveling companions. The problem is she is a vegetarian minimalist and I am a meat and potatoes abstract. She wants to buy a small trailer that looks like a fiberglass egg. I want an old 35 ft. school bus. Can you explain to her that people do not live full-time in such a small space? I have tried to explain to her that we need the kind of room that a big bus offers. She insists that it is doable and I cannot reason with her. Please send help.

—About to be Crammed in Camden

Dear Crammed:

I am a bit suspect of your motives. Are you hooking up with this woman for companionship or a social security check and Golden Age campground passport? You haven't enlightened me on what you have in common but it is obviously not camping style. There are several small trailer brands that fit the fiberglass egg description. One of the more popular is the Casita. It is small and practical and people do full-time RV in them. They make travel fuel efficient, have very functional floor plans and utilize every square inch of space to the maximum. An old school bus, on the other hand, would be far from fuel efficient and most likely more expensive to turn into a comfortable RV. I would have to agree with your companion between the two choices you have offered. It will be a close relationship, and I am talking quarters, not compassion. Much of the storage available when hauling a trailer this size will be in the tow vehicle. You might want to pack light in the beginning so that you will have less to carry if she ends up dropping you off along the highway. You must face the fact that this idea will always be in the back of her head. Think about it. Without you, she doubles the size of her trailer living space and most likely has twice as much money.

—Keep Smilin', Dr. R.V. Shrink

Just passing through Hope, Arizona can be an experience in itself

Campground Quiet Time "NOT"

Dear Dr. R.V. Shrink:

We have been RVing for a long time but recently we had an event that was a new experience for us. I thought we had seen it all, but I was wrong. We were in Silver River State Park in Florida and about ten o'clock at night a group showed up to claim the site next to us. They were camping in a horse trailer with a loud diesel truck as a tow vehicle. Without exaggeration, it took them over an hour to back it into a wide, straight site, with little to hit except bushes. For a while, I thought it must be the Candid Camera crew trying to get a stir out of us. It was all I could do to keep my husband from going out and parking it for them. They were yelling, "Whoa, stop, hold it, go forward, back to the left, you're crooked" and before they were done a few other choice words. I thought it was humorous after a while but my husband could hardly stand it. I told him it was all part of the camping experience and that on occasion we would have to deal with stupid people who are clueless when it comes to common sense and quiet manners. He thinks he needs to give classes to those who haven't figured it out on their own yet. I think that can be dangerous in this day and age. Can you throw in your two cents?

—Coiled Spring in Silver Springs

Dear Coiled:

You have to think of those occasions as experiences. You now have a great story to tell around the campfire when you are with fellow campers. Trust me, you have yet to see it all. If you let every inconsiderate camper annoy you to the point of distraction you will take years off your camping life. Campground life is not a utopian existence, but in my opinion, it is close. You will experience a good, even wonderful outcome 95% of the time. You can improve those odds as you travel more and learn which camping areas offer less chance of having a close neighbor. Just be thankful you don't own real estate next to people like the ones you experienced at Silver River. You can always move to another campsite when things become unmanageable. Some folks have no clue how to back up a rig, but a quiet campground in the dark is no time to learn. Give everyone the benefit of the doubt, you never know what they might have been through before they made it to your quiet little oasis that night. Patience is a virtue.

    —Keep Smilin', Dr. R.V. Shrink

RV Mother-in-Law Apartment

Dear Dr. R.V. Shrink:

    We have had a large motorhome for many years. I always thought that after I retired, my wife and I would travel several months during the year. Now that I have retired and have all my ducks in a row, my wife refuses to go because her 83-year-old mother would be left alone. My mother-in-law is healthy and active but my wife is afraid she would feel abandoned if we were gone that long. Can you give me some suggestions on how to convince my wife we need to have a life too? I love my mother-in-law but I don't want to miss traveling in our golden years because she might need us occasionally. Any help would be greatly appreciated.

    —Mommy-in-Law's Boy in Bowling Green

Dear Mommy's Boy:

    If you really love your mother-in-law, take her along. There is a large percentage of boomers who have parents to care for. I think that is an honorable responsibility in most cases. If you have a large motorhome and everyone gets along, why not travel with mom if she is willing. It's like a mother-in-law apartment on wheels. I have seen this work out wonderfully in many traveling relationships. It sometimes takes a while to work out all the scheduling bugs between a couple and a parent all living in a small space, but it is very feasible. With cell phones, email and even Skype, on today's portable computers, it is easy to stay in touch with loved ones while traveling. Those devices do not replace spending quality time with an aging parent. Another plus could be having a live-in referee. I know one couple, both with Type A personalities, that seem to argue all the time. Once her mother joined them on the road it mellowed them both out, added a third voice to the conversation, and they often used her for the tie-breaking vote involving important decisions. This third wheel relationship is not going to work for everyone. Don't make any rash moves until you consider all the negatives that could positively drive you to drink. Good Luck

—Keep Smilin', Dr. R.V. Shrink

Sometimes you end up camping right next to a Jackass

RV Mobile Connection Conflicts

Dear Dr. R.V. Shrink:

My wife and I are finding we rely more and more on our computer internet connection while traveling. We use it for directions, campground reservations, fuel prices, weather forecasting, hiking info, banking, emailing and the list goes on. The problem recently is we both want to be on at the same time. She says I look over her shoulder like a hawk waiting to snag a field mouse. I think we should have set hours that each of us claims as our time to surf the net. She says that is too restrictive. What would you suggest? I'm tired of feeling guilty about using this great resource when

she also wants to be online. Thanks in Advance.
—Webel Rouser in Washington State

Dear Webel:

How much is it worth for you to solve your problem? All you need is a wireless router to plug your Air Card into and you and your wife can both be on at the same time if you have two devices that will access the internet. I get many questions about computer sharing so let me give you some examples of what others do to solve the problem. If you only have one laptop you will need a second device. You might consider a smaller notebook, used laptop, IPAD, iPod, iPhone or any number of choices available. If you have a cell phone service provider, they will be offering a data package. With Verizon, for example, you pay about $60/mo. for 5G of data. They also offer a WiFi device for sharing the connection. If you already have an air card you can buy a wireless router that the card plugs into from companies like Cradlepoint. Remember, when you are both on at the same time you will be eating up data at twice the rate. I don't want you to solve one argument just to create another over your next cellular bill. Another frustration RVer's experience is weak connections. You can solve some of that with a product like Wilson Electronic signal booster kits. They do help. All this technology costs money, but it will pay for itself quickly if you find cheaper camping, fuel, and better directions. It's all part of fine-tuning your RV travel lifestyle. Many changes are just over the horizon and a computer and internet connection are becoming more important every year. So stop fighting over the computer and work together at beefing up your online capabilities. The only problem with all this easy access connectivity is your relatives always know where to find you.
—Keep Smilin', Dr. R.V. Shrink

RV Road Rage

Dear Dr. R.V. Shrink:

I have an ongoing problem with road rage. He sits right next to me in the motorhome and swears a blue streak at the outside world as we drive down the road. If we are in rural areas he seems like a perfectly normal, compassionate human being. When we get into heavy traffic congestion, construction zones or have to turn around because of a missed turn, he goes nutso! I think he needs a course in anger management, but he tells me he is working on a home remedy to "just say no" to spells of frustration and the rage that follows. Can you help us? Is this a normal RV symptom? I see rigs much larger than our Class "C" with a "toad." I can't hear into the cockpit of those rigs. Maybe everyone is raging on down the road. Let me know what you think and what I should do to combat my husband's road hostilities.

—Blue Streak in Biloxi

Dear B S:

I think this is more common than many people like to admit. You don't hear this often in campground conversation, but you can bet it is more common than people let you believe. Many drivers are capable but not comfortable towing a large rig. I know a retired tour bus driver that spent his career driving 40 ft. Tour buses into New York City and Boston but couldn't get used to pulling a 30 ft. Fifth wheel. I met another woman who couldn't stand to listen to her husband swear and talk to other drivers that irritated him. She bought him a sound device that made various weapon sounds. He would use his machine gun or rocket launcher sounds to vent his frustrations. It is no different from trying to kick a smoking habit. You have to want to quit and work hard at keeping your wits about you. Another thought would be to have your husband pull off to the side of the road immediately and do some deep breathing, yoga relaxation poses and make various meditative sounds to connect his RV spirit to the primordial OM sounds resonating throughout the universe. Relaxing and building mental capacity for patience is the key. Rage can ruin a trip, cause unhealthy stress, become a safety issue and ruin a traveling relationship. You may want to do some of the driving when you see your husband going off the deep end. That will be his signal that he is going too far. It may help him put his actions into perspective and mellow him out a bit.

—Keep Smilin', Dr. R.V. Shrink

Lost Dutchman State Park in Arizona

RV Shakedown Cruise

Dear Dr. R.V. Shrink:

My wife gets irritated with me every time we start out on a trip. We recently headed south with our Class "C" motorhome and the morning we left it was below zero. Everything was frozen. I lost my two front hubcaps somewhere along the highway the first morning. My starting battery was being ornery. When we hit warm weather and I could add water, the hot water heater wouldn't kick on. After an hour I found the problem to be the reset button. Now I am sitting on the Florida surf and my air conditioning, that I just spent $500 dollars repairing, isn't working. It seems like every time we leave there are several problems to solve. I make sure all systems are go before I store the rig, but it never fails to challenge me the first few days on the road. My wife thinks it's just me. She says, "It's Murphy's Law, and Murphy is shadowing you all the time." Don't other people have these same problems? Is it me? Am I just not cut out for the RV lifestyle? Any help would be greatly appreciated.

—Murph the Surf in Sarasota

Dear Murph:

Don't sweat it, buddy. The first few days out with your rig is called the "Shakedown Cruise." Everybody has your same problems. Often a rig that sits, develops more problems than one that is in constant operation. You should think of your problems as an educational experience. Remember, "Adversity builds character." Every time you work through a problem, it becomes one more notch on your maintenance gun. Next time you will know exactly what is wrong or be able to help someone else figure it out. My guess is that you have snap on wheel covers.

Don't replace them. You can buy the bolt on covers for less money and not have to worry about losing them every time some tire jockey works on your rig and doesn't replace them properly. Add valve extensions at the same time if you haven't already. Checking tire pressure often will save you money in the long run. I am going to guess that when you left home you were doing big miles every day trying to reach warmer weather. Long days of driving can be stressful, especially when things are not all functioning properly. The right mental attitude is everything. Begin a trip realizing that you are going to have some mechanical challenges. It's all part of the adventure.

—Keep Smilin', Dr. R.V. Shrink

Loading the RV in Winter

Dear Dr. R.V. Shrink:

I'm getting the cold shoulder from my wife. She doesn't like the winter weather we have here in Minnesota and always wants to pack the motorhome and head south in November. I'm an avid ice fisherman and I can't do that in Arizona, so I prefer to leave around the middle of February and enjoy the spring desert. The big problem always arises when we start to load our RV in February. She refuses to help. She told me this morning while I was taking a load out to the motorhome, "If we left in November we wouldn't have five feet of snow to deal with." It didn't help that we were having another blizzard. I know she still loves me. She tied a rope around my waist. That way, if I got lost in the blizzard, it would be easier for her to find me—in the spring. Do you think

I'm inconsiderate Doc? Should I leave for Arizona in November and just read about ice fishing in Outdoor Life? I thought leaving in February was a happy medium, but obviously, my wife thinks different. Please help me handle this difficult situation.

—Ice Hole in Bemidji

Dear Ice Hole:

I wouldn't call late February a happy medium. That's almost spring in Minnesota. Most snowbirds are thinking about heading home by then. In Quartzsite, they have started rolling up the sidewalks. It may not help your loading task, but you could get your fishing in earlier than that and head out the middle of January. That would be more of a compromise. If the weather keeps turning the way it's been this past couple of years, you should be able to ice fish in Arizona soon. Until then I would leave a bit earlier and have the motorhome pre-loaded as much as possible. Look for sales and outfit the motorhome with items that stay in the rig. That way, when you get ready to pull anchor, you throw in some last minute items and you're "back on the road again." Think like a firefighter. Another option, if financially feasible, would be to leave in November and fly home for the holidays and fit in some ice fishing at that time. You and your wife need to work out a plan that meets both your needs. I think late February puts you on thin ice.

—Keep Smilin', Dr. R.V. Shrink

Tutelage

RV Stale Mate

Dear Dr. R.V. Shrink:

We sold our house six years ago, bought a Class A motorhome and hit the road. We have had a wonderful journey. We have been all over North America. Having that experience under our belt I think we are a bit spoiled. Things seem to be changing. It is harder to get into campgrounds, the price is skyrocketing on gas and camping. The government keeps trying to take away the few camping benefits we have and it just doesn't seem as enjoyable as I originally remember it. I want to buy some property in the Southwest and spend the winters in one spot and my husband wants to keep moving all the time. My plan would still give us all summer to head for cooler climes and even spring and fall for places we love in the southern tier states. This has been an ongoing debate for over a year now and we are still moving every 7 to 10 days. Can you shed some light on how I should approach this dilemma?

—Stale Mate in Big Bend

Dear Stale:

It happens. Life is like that. Remember when you were a kid

and everything was a new adventure? Living life takes the polish off many new and exciting experiences. That's a good thing. You need to spice up your life again. Shake things up. If you have done all the things you dreamed of in North America, why not park the rig next winter and rent one in Australia or New Zealand. North America has not cornered the RV market. You might want to try RVing Europe in the summer. I think buying a piece of dirt in a warm climate is a great idea and a good investment. Many people find a little piece of paradise, build the camping site they always dreamed of and even a storage building for storing the RV while they are off on other adventures. You can also add a few sites for friends. I don't have to tell you that you make wonderful friends while roaming. It's great to have a place you can all gather on occasion. So I don't see a problem here unless your husband won't bend at all. I think you can both have what you want, build some equity in a piece of real estate and see more of this glorious planet we live on. If foreign travel is not your thing, I think you are offering your spouse a workable option. He gets to travel a majority of the year and you get your nesting time in one spot during the winter. Life is a compromise. I think if you two have survived in a motorhome for six years you have the right stuff. I am confident you will make the needed adjustments to continue your wonderful journey.

—Keep Smilin', Dr. R.V. Shrink

Ruth the RV Ranger

Dear Dr. R.V. Shrink:

My wife Ruth and I are both retired and started living half the year in our travel trailer in the warmer climates of the U.S. My wife has always been very active and loves our travels, but she found herself bored after a couple of years of sight-seeing. We are not commercial park types. We like natural settings in the varied parklands of America. Ruth started volunteering during the winter and now wants to start a new career with the Interior Department. She found a backcountry ranger position and wants to pursue it this summer. I am arguing against it. We still have a home to maintain, we have plenty of income and now I see myself spending my summers waiting for her to get off work. She volleys back that we will be living in a National Park. Am I wrong in not wanting to get tied down to one location for several months a year while Ruth pursues her new occupation and I stay home alone?

—Ranger Ruth's Spouse in Ruidoso

Dear Lone Ranger:

Let me begin with the fact that you are not the Lone Ranger. Many people who retire and begin a traveling lifestyle as you did, find a new passion along the way. Many times that takes the form of a job. It is often not a financial necessity. Your question does not surprise me. The National Park System and now many state and local parks cannot survive without the ever-growing army of volunteers. These volunteer jobs often network into full-time paying positions. The flexibility of retired and semiretired RVer's is a perfect match for the park service. It sounds like you two have different ideas on how to divide your time between home and travel, work and play. This is something you will have to work out in your own personal relationship. After a good healthy debate, one of you must yield to the other's wishes. I would suggest you give it a shot for a year. If you enjoy the natural areas, perhaps you will find plenty to do once you settle into a given park and have ample time to explore it. Your wife may find a big difference between a flexible volunteer job and a time-consuming, often stressful, full-time ranger position. If you don't let her give it a try she will always wonder. Life is an adventure. You may discover this new arrangement suits you and expands your retirement horizon. You might compromise with agreeing to try it for a season or two and then reevaluating the decision. Don't be ruthless or you'll be Ruth-less.

    —Keep Smilin', Dr. R.V. Shrink

Sunset in Big Bend Country

Positive Attitude on Negative RV Rodent Problem

Dear Dr. R.V. Shrink:

My wife and I have a 30 ft. motorhome worth over a hundred grand. We are not using it this winter and I have it stored in the yard in a canvas portable garage. I have a problem with rodents moving in and spending the winter exploring and chewing wire coatings. I want to bait heavily with Decon but my wife is totally against it. She has put mint tea leaves around and some questionable high-frequency sound machine that is supposed to drive them away. She feels that the mice will be eaten by our resident raptors and the poison will be transmitted to them. I still find signs of mice and want to bait for them. This has caused several heated arguments. Can you bring some common sense to this issue before I need a full-time electrician to rewire my rig? —Positively Negative in New Hampshire Dear + -I think I can make you both happy campers. This is a common problem and can become expensive and frustrating very quickly next time you go to use your rig and find a mouse nest in your converter or on your engine block. Rodents are attracted to the coating on the many miles of wire that travel through a rig, creating electrical shorts. If that is not enough reason, they just plain like to chew stuff. What you need to do is stop arguing and put that energy into a quick and easy recycling craft project. Get a couple 5-gallon plastic buckets, a few recycled soup cans and a length of wire. Punch a hole in the bottom center of the cans. Duct tape two together at the opened end. String the wire through the holes and twist it off on both sides of the bucket top. Fill the bucket with RV antifreeze. Spread some peanut butter on the soup cans and strategically place your new mouse trap in and/or around your rig. You can place a stick up to the bucket to make it easy for any rodents that desire a little peanut butter. They will step out on the cans which will quickly spin them off into the water/antifreeze solution and quickly drown. This is much more humane than poison, much quicker and continues to work all season. Your wife can still continue with her system. If it does work there will be no casualties. If it doesn't you have a guaranteed backup line of defense.

   —Keep Smilin', Dr. R.V. Shrink

Needy RV Neighbors

Dear Dr. R.V. Shrink:

   We have been full-time RVing for about seven years. We have met many wonderful people. However, occasionally we meet a stalker. It is usually a single person, perhaps lonely. The latest example happened in the Everglades National Park at Flamingo Campground. I called him "Ears." My husband could not step foot out of our motorhome before this fellow camper was Johnny on the spot. He had to be sitting at his trailer window watching for my husband to exit. It was almost funny if not so annoying. My husband was very patient and spent time letting this guy shadow him and talk his ear off, but finally, we moved to another campground ahead of schedule because it became too annoying. Should we have stayed and explained to this person that we needed less contact? It was very awkward. We kept looking in the rearview mirror as we headed north to see if we were being tailed. —An Earful in FloridaDear Earful: The answer would depend on how flexible you are. I applaud your husband's patience. Some people are lonely and need a listening post. However, there must be some limitations. If the person is rude, irritating, nosey or inconsiderate in some way, I would have no problem setting them straight. First with some subtle hints, and if that didn't work, being more direct.

Sometimes you do not have the convenience of moving. Perhaps you have paid in advance for a long-term space. Each instance would be a judgment call on the annoying scale of one to ten. I think you will agree in your seven years of living the RV lifestyle, the majority of the people you connect with are a joy, not a hassle. A huge part of this lifestyle is meeting interesting people from all walks of life. That is not to say that you have to spark with every camping neighbor you meet. This is no different than any other relationship problem you encounter in life. Make good judgments and watch your rearview mirror.

   —Keep Smilin', Dr. R.V. Shrink

Camping in New Mexico High Country

Old story for young in RV parks

Dear Dr. R.V. Shrink:

We are not your average couple. We are in our late 20's and traveling full-time. We are not rich. We are working our way around the country. We live in a vintage 28 ft. Avion. We didn't want to wait until retirement to do this. We have no children yet and decided to travel for a year. Five years later we are still at it. Our problem is age bias. We find, especially in the popular winter destinations, many of the parks are 55 and older parks. They don't come right out and say it, but we can never seem to find a spot in a park near where we find a job because we are too young. Once we talk a park into letting us stay, they love us. Last winter my husband, who is quite mechanically inclined, ended up fixing dozens of problems people had with their rigs. We go to all the potlucks and pitch in when we are not working. We are quiet and tidy. How can we convince park managers of this without flashing an AARP card?

—The Young and the Restless in Apache Jct.

Dear Restless:

You are not the problem, but it sounds like you are the solution. You are unfortunately being categorized into a slot you obviously do not belong. In defense of the park management, they are trying to create a harmonious group of winter residents that all fit a specific slot. I am sure you understand that a majority of people your age might not be on the same schedule as those retired. Park management can have problems with anyone who drives through the gate, but you come with a big question mark that screams the possibility of loud music, parties, work schedules and various interests that might put you out of step with the rest of the group. I think you seem to be representing yourself as capable and flexible enough to fit in. I think you should challenge the situation head-on. Answer all the questions the park management is not asking you when you first make your pitch. Put their mind at rest. Have an agreement up front as to behaviors expected. If possible give references to parks you have already spent winters in. Then write and tell me where you are staying. I have a few cockpit problems with my rig I would like your husband to fix.

—Keep Smilin', Dr. R.V. Shrink

Full-Timing in an RV with cats

Dear Dr. R.V. Shrink:

We are thinking about buying a large Class A motorhome. My husband and I want to travel full-time for a few years. We have been planning this for some time. We read a lot of RV magazines and blogs and I see that many full-timers have pets. My husband doesn't think that is a good idea. We have two cats and they are my babies. I don't plan to travel without them and he doesn't plan to travel with them. We are at a roadblock before we even get on the road. Can you offer any constructive advice to convince him that I am right? They are indoor cats and would never have to leave the motorhome. The units we have looked at so far have huge storage bays that are accessible from inside the coach. One would be perfect for food litter and bedding. Please help me.

—Catastrophe in Columbus

Dear Columbus:

There is no sense in having a catfight before you even take the brake off. Traveling pets are as common as a cold. I would estimate that at least 50 percent of the people I meet on the road have a pet traveling with them. This rig is going to be your "home" on the road, and there is no place like home for a cat or dog that gives you company. I can vouch for the no hassle addition of having two cats travel with you. My wife and I have done it for years. One likes to help navigate from the front window and the other makes a beeline for the storage bay (cat cave) if I so much as look at the driver's seat. I have to admit that they will escape on occasion. We have always found them and persuaded them to rejoin us. Actually, you will meet a lot of wonderful people while looking for a missing cat in a campground. I would suggest you have your husband read some of the articles you have found pertaining to traveling cats. It is truly not like trying to give a cat a bath. You will find them to have an adventuresome spirit. You don't have to walk them at dark-thirty, they bury their own land mines and you can leave them "home alone" for a couple of days. They are very responsible and know how to take care of themselves. All cats, big and small, sleep on average, eighteen hours a day. They don't bark, and best of all you can take them into any park because you don't even have to declare them.

—Keep Smilin,' Dr. R.V. Shrink

Boarding the Zion National Park shuttle bus
next to the campground

RV parking at Walmart

Dear Dr. R.V. Shrink:

We have been using Walmart parking lots for overnight stays
while traveling between destinations. We think this is a wonderful
opportunity offered by Walmart. We call them our "Pit Stops."
We do our shopping, laundry nearby and rent a movie from Red
Box. They always have an out-of-the-way area that is not too
noisy or bright. Several times we have noticed other campers not
just taking advantage of a good thing, but potentially ruining it

for the rest of us. We have seen people with tables and chairs out under their awning, small fenced in dog pens erected, large generators in the parking lot next to the rig running loud and smoky, tents and loud arguments over parking spaces. It takes every tactical maneuver I can muster to keep my husband from turning into a Walmart referee. He wants so badly to go over and give them a piece of his mind. He thinks he is Wyatt Earp. I tell him I didn't start traveling to put up with non-campground conflict. If it bothers him so much I think we should avoid these overnight stays. Besides, I think it could be dangerous confronting people that obviously have no common sense. He loves your column and I think if he hears some advice from you he may listen. Thanks in advance.

—Up Against the Wall-mart in Earp, CA

Dear Up:

Don't get down on your husband. Those kinds of irresponsible actions can make sane people crazy. I agree he should not try to be the "Law West of the Walmart." I also agree that these people do jeopardize the convenience we all enjoy. Walmart has actually been challenged by interests that would like to see them discontinue overnight parking privileges. They refused to stop offering this service. They said it was another customer service they would continue to promote in locations that did not disallow it by city ordinance. One thing you can do, to help compensate for the inconsiderate few who abuse the service, is be a loyal, courteous customer. Let store management know you are shopping and thank them for allowing you to stay. Call ahead and ask permission, even if you know it is allowed. Often they like RV's to congregate in a certain section of the parking lot. Also, things change and you never know when a new ordinance might restrict overnight parking. These are much better tactics than confrontation with parking lot neighbors. If your husband goes out at all be sure to have him check his guns at the door. If anything, let him walk around the parking lot with a very large, official looking badge and stare, but, make him promise he won't talk to anyone.

—Keep Smilin', Dr. R.V. Shrink

Motorhome Brake Dancing

Dear Dr. R.V. Shrink:

Maybe you can help solve this constant problem my wife and I have every time we park our rig. It's a little embarrassing but I know many other people suffer from the same situation. We both drive our motorhome, we both take turns dumping the septic, we both know how to troubleshoot all the appliances. We are a great team. The problem is, she thinks she's an expert at backing up and parking the rig. She is always telling others that I'm terrible at it. The fact is, I just give better signals than she does. I can get behind the motorhome and maneuver her right into the tightest spots with good hand signals. When I'm driving, I can't even see her in the mirrors. She is usually in a blind spot behind the rig, flapping her hands and her gums. While she's back there dancing around I can't see or hear her. We have discussed this problem a million times, but I still can't get it through to her where to stand and what signals I need. Any help would be greatly appreciated.

—Brake Dancing in Denver

Dear Brake:

This is a huge problem. I hear this constantly. If you look around the campground as people arrive you will see this scenario played out time and again. Couples seem to get frustrated with each other when trying to work together to park, especially in tight spaces. I suggest patience. Armed with that I suggest a couple of props. The first is very important—an oven mitt. Yes, you heard me right. This is most important. If the person behind the rig giving parking signals wears an oven mitt there are certain signals that will not be able to be seen no matter how frustrated that person becomes. This can go a long way toward keeping the peace until the rig finally gets parked. Another piece of equipment that comes in handy is a cheap pair of walkie-talkies. You can often find them at second-hand stores for a few bucks. Another problem I see, in a majority of parking conflict cases, is over politeness. Not between the couple but with blocking traffic. Don't worry about blocking the road or holding up another camper. We are all in the same boat (land yacht). They don't mind waiting for you to take your time and get parked properly. Just don't let them help you. Remember, they don't have anything invested. Your spouse is going to make sure you don't impale your rig on some hidden branch, but a bystander may not be as concerned. The next time you park the rig make a conscious effort to hold your tongue. Remember, it's in a slippery spot. Make a pact, no fighting over parking. Watch others and see just how silly it is, then put yourself in that picture. Your New Year's Resolution should be, "I'll watch your back-up, you watch mine."

—Keep Smilin', Dr. R.V. Shrink

My parents retired and traveled
with a 31 ft. Airstream for many years

Down in the RV Dumps

Dear Dr. R.V. Shrink:

We have been on our first shakedown cruise with a new class C
motorhome. It has been a real eye-opening, learning experience.
I have always taken my waste disposal for granted. I flush the
toilet and it disappears forever. Now I get to see it one more time
before it goes off to the big sewage system in the great unknown.
My problem is not sanitation. I am questioning dump station

manners. In my opinion, so far they stink. My first experience was outside Cody, Wyoming. It was a free dump station near a Veteran's Memorial Park. The sign clearly stated "No Commercial Dumping." Halfway through my dumping process, a Canadian Tour bus pulled in. The driver backed up to the hole on his side (this was a two-holer) while his tour guide positioned him over the target. I could not imagine they were going to pull the pin without at least hooking up a hose. When I finally figured out that's exactly what they were going to do, I screamed to my wife, "Jump or swim." We hopped in the rig and sped off just as they pulled the plug. I was so upset I went a little ballistic. I walked back over to the dump station and told them what I thought about their method and inconsideration as we were standing just a few feet away. This is the most extreme example I can list so far, but I am just starting. My wife says I should roll with the punches and not let these people set me off. Should I suffer in silence when I find myself dumping with dopes, or relieve my stress by giving them a little "crap" so to speak?

—Bob in Blackwater, VA

Dear Bob:

First, I think you made the right decision. Always run first. I think you will find most fellow RV'ers to be very polite when it comes to sharing dumping stations. Most will go the extra mile when it comes to cleaning the area before they leave. Unfortunately, there are always a few bad apples that spoil the barrel. I don't think losing your temper will make these people act or smell any better. For every dump station user that soils the area you will find nine that leave the area clean and tidy. Seldom will you be up against a tour bus worth of waste. Most RV'ers are using dump stations in a campground setting. I looked your dump station

up on the internet. Yes, the internet can even tell you where to take a dump (rvdumps.com). You were at a city dump station that was probably there for the convenience of campers like yourself. Even if these jokers you had to deal with had permission, they still should have been more considerate and squared away, hygienically speaking. Losing your temper in the scenario you described is very understandable. In normal conditions, let it go. No pun intended.
—Keep Smilin', Dr. R.V. Shrink

RV Insurance—Never Leave Home Without It!

Dear Dr. R.V. Shrink:

We just bought a new Montana 5th wheel last month and escaped the Michigan Siberian north. We are in a great park in Bradenton Beach, Florida and feel we made the right decision. Having a new rig is exciting but I think my husband worries about it too much. We are well insured but have seen two hit and runs already this month. They are not malicious attacks. These people probably don't even know they had hit something until they discovered a dent in their rigs. Our neighbor with a 40-foot motorhome, pulling a small pickup truck, pulled out while we were eating breakfast one morning. He took out a small palm tree on our site and just missed our truck. Before he exited the park he went over the curb and scraped a fire hydrant. He never even realized he hit anything. Two days later the couple across the street with a three axle Airstream wiped out the whole side of their trailer, wrapping it around a telephone pole while turning out of their site too sharply. This morning while out walking we saw another motorhome back into a car while leaving the park. Is this a common occurrence for RVers? I hate to have my husband dwell on this issue all the time. I keep telling him it is just chance that we have witnessed so many collisions in the short time we have been traveling. He is already designing a portable post system to border our campsites as a "first line of defense" as he calls it. Please tell me this is not necessary. I feel like we are spending too much time worrying about this issue instead of enjoying our surroundings. I feel like my husband is getting to the point where he is not comfortable leaving our rig unattended.

—Bump and Grind in Bradenton

Dear Bumper:

Don't worry. Be happy. When you look around the campground at some of the large rigs that now ply the road, you would think this could be a huge problem. If you go on the internet and look for RV accident statistics you will find very little information. The fact is, RVers don't hurt enough people to warrant their own statistic. I think your above average accident witnessing will decrease as you continue to travel. Look optimistically at your experience so far. It has heightened your personal awareness and will make you more careful in your own towing practice. When someone has a good percentage of their net worth in a new comfortable home on wheels, it makes them ever conscious of their surroundings and driving habits. Many dealers take new customers through a driving course to demonstrate turning radius, swing ratio and tips on using mirrors effectively. Each driver is unique. This is no different from learning to drive a light truck or van. Each type of RV has a different reaction while maneuvering around tight campgrounds. I have known tour bus drivers who would take a 40-foot tour bus into New York City but could not get used to parking a 5th wheel. Your husband should hold off on his "Perimeter Pole" design until you have had more time to experience just how safe it is to be surrounded by a whole herd of various sized RV's. There is a "One-Eyed" guy I wrote about a few weeks ago you might want to be aware of. Otherwise, I think you will discover the wonderful world of RV travel is almost utopia like in the safety department. You should encourage your husband to leave your rig unattended for extended lengths of time until his paranoia has sufficiently eased. Enjoy all of your neighbors and never, I mean never, let them see you sweat!

—Keep Smilin', Dr. R.V. Shrink

Driving Mr. Boo across North Dakota
"Are we there yet Dad?"

Campground Reservation Dilemma

Dear Dr. R.V. Shrink:

My wife and I are fairly new at RVing. We didn't realize how difficult it was going to be to secure a campsite when and where we travel. The reality of this time-consuming chore never entered our minds during the years we dreamed of roaming around North America in our travel trailer. It has taken The adventure out of our sails. Our utopian plans of throwing out the anchor wherever the wind blew us has turned into the nightmare of securing reservations well in advance and putting ourselves on a schedule. We thought our time clock days were behind us and now find ourselves rat-racing around and keeping a daily planner again. Is this a syndrome that many Rver's suffer with or will we finally overcome our fear of being site-less and end up in long lines with people that refuse to be sent to the reservation system?

—Dan in Demming

Dear Dan:

It's a fact of life. A majority of campgrounds have become bookie joints. The future holds more of the same. You can let it corral you or use it to your advantage. It is not a perfect world we have created. The old saying, "If given lemons, make lemonade," applies here to your feelings. The realities of the road are often much different from the picture ads you have been drooling over for years. That said, it is still a wonderful lifestyle. You have to weigh the difference of planning your trip far in advance and knowing you have secure sites, or winging it and taking your chances. The deck is stacked against you if you decide to wing it. There are actually scalpers who buy up the best sites and seasons in many state and national parks and resell them in bidding auctions on eBay and Craigslist. In Florida, for example, many state parks have gone completely to reservations. Even if you do find a site during the week, you often have to move out on the weekend because they have been completely booked months in advance. Many National Forest Campgrounds have gone to reservations. I wouldn't be surprised if soon it won't be necessary to book ahead at Camp Walmart. The boondocking days are dwindling. It's a numbers game we call supply and demand. Many places that used to be free are now charging for two reasons — #1 because they can, and #2 because of overuse. In the present economy, you will find many free campgrounds full of unfortunate people who have lost their homes to foreclosure. There have already been attempts to erode the Senior Discount from government campgrounds, and with state budgets, in the black water tank, you are finding fewer services and less maintained facilities at higher fees. My advice is to stop dwelling on lemons and adjust the sails and make lemonade. There are still many wonderful places to drop anchor. You can arm yourself with more information using campground directories, computer websites, fellow campers, and news media to find those gems that few have discovered. Eventually, you will find places appealing enough and you will know when you want to return and for how long. At that point "Book 'em Danno," and you will end up loving the reservation system.

—Keep Smilin', Dr. R.V. Shrink

Campground Segregation

Dear Dr. R.V. Shrink:

I am seeking help with a problem I have had ever since I started full-time RVing. I am single and I have a wonderful little rig. I pull a 17 foot Casita with an older model Jeep Wrangler Laredo. I have developed a complex over the past several years about my size. Everyone seems to believe that size matters. I don't feel bigger is better, but in many situations, I am treated as small and insignificant. I love to Kayak and carry an inflatable 12' Sea Eagle kayak. I prefer to camp near the water and I am finding that many parks reserve their water sites strictly for larger and newer rigs than mine. It seems discriminatory. I am willing to pay the value added price for the water sites, but the big dogs do not seem to want me hanging out with them. I was recently in Florida on the Ocklawaha River at a wonderful campground. The river sites were 25 percent more money. I was willing to pay but was informed that I was "too small." There were sites available but the neighborhood was occupied only by monster motorhomes in the several hundred thousand dollar range. I can afford to buy a comparable rig with pocket change, like those taking up the primo spaces, but I prefer my small, unique, reliable, uncomplicated Casita. Do you suggest I get professional help or buy Psychology for Dummies on Amazon? I feel I need to deal with this malady soon. If I don't nip it in the bud it could end up taking over my life as increasingly more campgrounds become elitist country clubs.

—David in Goliath, Ga.

Dear David:

You need to concentrate on the phrase "Small Is Beautiful." This phrase is believed to empower people more in contrast with phrases such as "bigger is better." Size does matter but why not "Less is More." Size matters to you in your choice of rig size. It also matters to those privileged river site residents. I see two scenarios evolving in the RV world. The first is the one you describe. Many campgrounds are developing themselves to cater only to the high-end RV set or segregating as you in your case. This could change radically as more people are opting for smaller and more fuel-efficient rigs since the economic crash and spiking oil prices. I personally find it offensive when I am denied a space in a campground because of the age or size of my rig. However, mental health is best maintained by rationalizing these social realities. I would not and do not hesitate to display my displeasure with campground owners who flagrantly tell me I am not good enough for some section of their park. You are as much of the economic engine that runs the ever-changing camping industry as anyone else. You vote with your dollars. Your dollars count as much as the devaluated dollars packed around in the pockets of those in the more luxurious rigs. Money talks and boycott walks. Don't get mad, get even. Segregation can only be slain by marching, right out the door and down the road to an equal opportunity campground. You must decide if you want to practice long-distance kayak carrying techniques or affirmative action. Just say no to your mental complex, stiffen your spine and follow the river to another campground. Letting this social injustice eat away at you will only take you to a mental state known professionally as "up a creek without a paddle."

    —Keep Smilin', Dr. R.V. Shrink

Cultivation

RV party animals

Dear Dr. R.V. Shrink:

Can you tell me what my attitude should be about noisy camp-ground neighbors? I seem passive in situations because I do not react visibly to emotions I might be feeling. My husband, on the other hand, would be considered aggressive. He can sometimes detonate without much provocation. When we are camping in our motorhome next to a rowdy bunch I like to think they are letting off steam in a party mode and we should just move to a quieter site. My husband thinks they are inconsiderate and demands that they tone their noise levels down. Several times this has put us dangerously close to physical confrontation. Often alcohol is a factor, especially during the holiday camping season. Do you think the way to handle these situations is to move, confront, or submit in quiet frustration?

—Nervous in New Haven

Dear Nervous:

I agree with your husband on the inconsiderate charge. However, confrontation will bring you nothing but grief. Moving is an option but that still does not solve the problems for others around the offensive site. You might first want to report the problem to a campground host or ranger if one is available. Most campgrounds have some basic noise and quiet hour rules. In most cases, these are good people, gone bad. As you say, they are on a camping weekend and letting off steam. That still does not give them license to irritate their camping neighbors. A better option than being aggressive would be to "kill them" with kindness. Introduce yourself in a friendly fashion and ask them if they could keep it down a little. From that introduction, you will quickly discover if they are good people, gone bad, or inconsiderate people you will need to report or move away from. One of the advantages of the RV lifestyle, unlike home ownership, is the ability to pick new neighbors as quickly as moving your rig. Let me stress that fighting fire with fire is not the answer to your frustration. Trying to out rowdy your rowdy neighbors with higher decibels will only escalate things. So put away the four-foot amplifiers hooked to your Bose Wave music system playing Luciano Pavarotti, turn off the generator, stop honking the horn, and move on down the road.

—Keep Smilin' Dr. R. V. Shrink

WIFE WITH WEIGHT PROBLEM

Dear Dr. R.V. Shrink:

My wife has a terrible weight problem. I am trying to change her lifestyle in an effort to reduce her weight. It has started to affect our motorhome mileage. We travel several months of the year and she feels she has to bring half of our worldly possessions along on every trip. I have debated with her endlessly about the seemingly

needless paraphernalia she totes along and never uses. It all falls on deaf ears. When I start in on a discussion of reduction she takes her hearing aid out and refuses to participate. We haul bikes we never ride, a sewing machine never plugged in, extra pots, pans and iron skillets that never boil or fry anything. The list goes on. I am at my wit's end. How can I persuade her to leave some of this anchor accumulation in port when we sail off down the road? It takes me several miles to get up to speed and I avoid mountain passes like the plague.
—Lead Bottom in Leavenworth

Dear Lead Bottom:

With a heavy heart, I read of your dilemma. Some individuals are born pack rats. I think you may have married one. It is my guess that you realized this trait in your wife long before you had a motorhome. Carrying too much weight can be not only an expensive mistake but a safety issue. I would do a few things immediately. First, approach the subject from a safety viewpoint and not from that of a minimalist. Then slip her a copy of Walden by Thoreau. if that helps, follow up with The Zen of Decluttered Packrattery. Watch the old "I Love Lucy" trailer episode with Lucy sneaking her rock collection into the trailer when Desi isn't looking. All of these subtle tactics should have a cumulative impact. You may see your wife begin to streamline her packing to a more frugal level of organization. In the meantime, you might want to make sure your holding tanks are as empty as you can keep them. Liquid is heavy and emptying your tanks will help you balance out your wife's perceived necessities and save on gas. Also, be sure your brakes are up to snuff. After exhausting all good faith efforts you will eventually have to say, "Enough is enough" and start throwing out ballast if you expect to rise from this dilemma. Motorhome obesity is the number one killer on steep, curvy, mountain roads. Your wife needs to understand the gravity of this situation. You may have to put your wife on a Weight Watcher program. Stop at every truck weigh station you come across and point out to her your above average scale ticket. It really comes down to health and safety issues. You need to balance this issue out before your next departure.

—Keep Smilin' Dr. R. V. Shrink

See you around the campfire
—KEEP SMILIN'

Geritol Posse Rides Again

Dear Dr. R.V. Shrink:

My wife and I spent a wonderful few days in one of Arizona's most beautiful "Sky Islands", high above Green Valley, Arizona. Being winter, we enjoyed sunny warm days and cold nights in Madera Canyon's Bog Springs National Forest Campground. We love these out of the way, hard to reach, NF campgrounds for the solitude they offer, the beautiful locations, and the dark quiet nights. The problem started when we left our mountain utopia and ventured into the valley below. The land of "Oscar the Grouch." We decided to stop at the Green Valley, AZ Library Book Sale to find some reading material. It was early in the morning and we found a huge mall type parking lot behind the library. The sign said it was the White Elephant Thrift Store, but other buildings looked like Sheriff, Road Commission, county type stuff. We were the only vehicle in the lot. I parked horizontally, taking up five spaces, way out at the edge of the lot in nobody's way. It was an hour until the library would open so we ate breakfast. Over the next hour, every lot slot in the parking area filled. We were amazed. A line was forming at the White Elephant Thrift door. Soon the Golden Girls blocked me in from the front and Archie and Edith blocked me in from the back. When the hundreds of lot slots were filled, people started parking out on both sides of the street. I thought I was just imagining the looks we were getting from people walking by. Could my five spaces be that important in a sea of overflowing vehicles that clearly had to flood the nearby roads whether I was squatting here or not? I went on a recon mission. I discovered they were all here for the White Elephant Thrift Store. It wasn't a once a year sale. This thing goes on six days a week, fifty-two weeks a year. It is more popular than Walmart at Christmas. When I got back to the motorhome I discovered I had not been imagining the "LOOK." The head of the Geritol Posse knocked at our door. At first, I thought it was the Sheriff. Brown shirt with official arm patches, khaki pants, shiny gold badge, and radio. My first clue she was White Elephant Security was the fact that she wasn't packin' any heat. She said, "You have to move. You are taking up five spaces." I could see the panic in my wife's face. She thought I was going to go into my raving jailhouse lawyer mode. It was true that I was breaking no law. I had every right to be parked where I was. I could have given this female Broderick Crawford much grief, but I could also see the strain in her face. Coming out and telling me I must move was the last thing she wanted to be doing, but the Golden Girls and several other complaints forced her from her better judgment. I could have unhooked, parked the car and motorhome separately and vertically. That would have really blocked the lot. I know that would have sent her into a panic. So instead of being Mr. Hyde, I decided to be Dr. Jekyll. I told her I couldn't squeeze out until she had one of her complainers move their vehicle. The word was out. I had been evicted. Cars were already vying for position to take my five spaces. When she got the car behind me moved, I still could not exit the parking lot until she made those crowding for the slots, like vultures on a fresh kill, move on past. They did not want to lose their positions. Because of poor eyesight, I could tell many had taken their Vytorin in combination with their Viagra at breakfast and it had hardened their hearts. They wanted to string me up but couldn't find a tall enough cactus. We finally eased on down the road and found a gas station that said we could drop the rig for a couple of hours. We went back to the library and later explored the White Elephant store. I saw my Rent-a-Cop friend and told her I had parked down in Nogales, Mexico and wondered if that was far enough. It still bothers me that I rolled over for this insinuated parking infraction. I feel I may have weakened RV Parking Rights when I cooperated and left my spaces. Should I have hunkered down, stood my ground, forced legal action for the benefit of all other RVer's who might need several spaces to park in the future? Am I getting soft? Could I be losing my debating will?

—Violated in Green Valley

Dear Violated:

There is no doubt that you had a rock solid case for parking where you were. I find it very compassionate on your part to accept the inconvenience of moving to relieve the stress of the security guard who had the thankless job of asking you to move. For you to recognize her uncomfortable situation and defuse it is commendable. I don't think this indicates you are losing your edge. Instead, you may be honing your relationship skills. If you never see that look of panic on your wife's face again, that could signal a soft patch in your abilities to dole out attitude adjustments to those in need. For any damage you might have inflicted on future RV Parking Rights, you more than made up for in goodwill with the Green Valley, White Elephant Law Enforcement Division of Arizona.

—Keep Smilin', Dr. R. V. Shrink

SLEEP APNEA CAMPING

Dear Dr. R.V. Shrink:

We have just started living the RV lifestyle and immediately the price of camping caused sticker shock. My husband now wants to do what he calls "stealth camping." He likes to park in crazy places when we are traveling that cost little or nothing. I know many people spend nights at Walmart and other retailers who seem fine with short-term camping, but my husband is now starting to look at hospital, church and VFW Hall parking lots as his personal KOA's. He claims "we pay our taxes" and pulls off into fields that he thinks are government-run public lands. I am as nervous as a squirrel in a bird feeder most of the time. I can't relax when we are parking in suspect spots. Maybe I watched too many horror films when I was young. Every time I hear a noise I think it's Eddie Scissorhands at the door asking us to leave. I swore, one night in Texas, I heard a chainsaw outside our rig. I keep telling him, "If we can't afford to stay in RV parks we shouldn't be traveling." Please give me some ammunition to argue my point. Often times I don't think we are safe.

   —Sleepless in Seattle

Dear Sleepless:

   Stealth Camping, Boon-Docking, or whatever else you want to call it, is fine to a point. It sounds like your husband might have an addiction to free camping. Safety should be your first priority. Walmart is a great pit stop when making time and looking for a safe harbor for the night. Most have security and welcome RV'ers for overnight parking. If your husband is insisting on staying in areas you feel are not safe, and it makes you feel uncomfortable, you need to let him know that you are not going to continue this practice. My suggestion would be to become effectively involved in finding reasonably priced RV sites. Use freecampgrounds.com, various campground books, start a database of nice places you find and places other campers tell you about. Most are not actually free, but very reasonable. Invest in discount camping services, get your senior camping pass from the government if you are seniors and

US citizens. Some states, for example, New Mexico, sell reasonable annual passes for state park camping. There is a whole host of ways to save money and camp in amazingly beautiful, safe places if you work at it. There is a difference between frugal and free. There is safety in numbers and usually, if it's a good idea, some other RV'er has already figured it out and will be there camped alongside you. If you are nervous about being asked to leave in the middle of the night, ask in advance. Many Walmarts will not allow overnight parking because of a City Ordinance. You have to help your husband understand that there is a difference between an RV'er and a person who is homeless. Don't let your husband sleep soundly while you are up all night worried about every little sound you hear. Wake him up and say, "Did you hear that?" He didn't, of course, because he was sleeping and there was no noise. After you do this a dozen times a night he will think twice about parking in places where you can't sleep.

—Keep Smilin', Dr. R. V. Shrink

Also by Richard Mallery

Made in United States
Orlando, FL
12 February 2022

14756400R00139